C0-DWH-740

Policy Issues in Education

Title entry

LA
210
.P64

Policy Issues in Education

PACIFIC UNIVERSITY LIBRARY
FOREST GROVE, OREGON

Edited by
Allan C. Ornstein
Steven I. Miller
Loyola University of Chicago

Lexington Books
D.C. Heath and Company
Lexington, Massachusetts
Toronto London

Library of Congress Cataloging in Publication Data

Main entry under title:
Policy issues in education.

1. Educational planning–United States–Addresses, essays, lectures. 2. Education and state–United States–Addresses, essays, lectures. I. Ornstein, Allan C. II. Miller, Steven I.
LA210.P64 379'.151'0973 75-36349
ISBN 0-669-00376-x

Copyright © 1976 by D.C. Heath and Company.

All rights reserved. No part of this publication may be reproduced or transmitted in any form or by any means, electronic or mechanical, including photocopy, recording, or any information storage or retrieval system, without permission in writing from the publisher.

Published simultaneously in Canada.

Printed in the United States of America.

International Standard Book Number: 0-669-00376-x

Library of Congress Catalog Card Number: 75-36349

Contents

List of Figure and Tables

Contributors

James E. Blackwell
University of Massachusetts, Boston

Raymond E. Cleveland
Texas A and M University

Virgil A. Clift
New York University

Patricia A. Craig
University of California, Berkeley

Robert L. Ebel
Michigan State University

James W. Guthrie
University of California, Berkeley

Martin Haberman
University of Wisconsin at Milwaukee

Harry L. Miller
Hunter College, City University of New York

Steven Miller
Loyola University of Chicago

Allan C. Ornstein
Loyola University of Chicago

Terry N. Saario
Ford Foundation, New York City

T.M. Stinnett
Texas A and M University

Ralph W. Tyler
Science Research Associates, Chicago

Introduction

No one book can provide sufficient information about policy issues regarding education. Whether an individual participates in educational decisions as a teacher, administrator, board member, parent, or concerned citizen, the issues to be resolved are difficult and complex. Policy makers prefer to use quantitative aspects of social science in the formation of educational decisions. The presumed exact and rational nature of the quantitative approach has inherent appeal to the policy makers in their attempt to order and audit political options and the implications of their choices.

Society is always changing, and as it changes the practices and processes of the schools must be modified to reflect the new conditions. Educational decisions must be made. In such a context, social scientists and educators link up with policy efforts—first, to satisfy the needs of society; second, to satisfy identifiable groups within society; and third, to satisfy individuals who themselves are largely without voice though they sometimes have the vote. The role of the social scientist and the educator involves *advocacy* and *analysis*, that is, they act to affect and shape policy.

Since policy affects people, people will try to exert all the influence they can to ensure that what emerges is in their best interests. Needless to say, special interest groups do not necessarily seek what is best for the larger society. Their goals do not necessarily make for good policy or for better educational and social programs, although much of the rhetoric of interest groups might have the public believe otherwise.

When deliberating upon education or social action, we should be aware of the political process. To say that educational systems are unpolitical is, at best, naive or, worse, dangerous since it blinds us to the reality of how policy is derived. In the same vein, all of us have a political framework in which we arrive at knowledge, systematize it, and organize it for "truth" and the causes of things. Although many social scientists and educators may claim objectivity and try to neutralize their biases, they invariably take a position for or against a specific policy. What is interpreted as facts and objective findings often coincides with a position that is comfortable to a group or an individual who is writing as a member of a group.

The contributors of this text are no different from other human beings; they have a set of biases and a viewpoint that characterize their statements and policy positions. Similarly, the reader is human, and the way he or she reacts to each chapter, for that matter any social-educational data, will reflect his or her position. With this in mind, we turn to some policy issues that impact on education. In doing so, we hope that this series of propositions are relevant today and can be generalized beyond this particular historical period.

Finally, the editors extend their thanks to each contributor who took time out from a busy schedule to write an original selection for this text. They represent a wide range of opinions: a liberal-conservative continuum, based geographically across the country and identified with various groups in society.

Part I: Evaluation Policies

Evaluation Policies

Policy making in education encompasses a large field of positions and insights. One of the most fundamental aspects has to do with the evaluation of policy from different perspectives. The policy maker is responsible, not only for formulating and implementing policy, but also for understanding the more technical aspects of the process. These include such things as testing, evaluation, and the use of empirical evidence.

While the educational policy maker may not be an expert in all areas, he or she is still responsible for knowing generally how the various aspects of the policy making process influence the type of decisions that will eventually be made. Without this knowledge, a policy maker is at a loss to determine whether his or her decision is the correct one in a given situation.

For example, if an educational policy maker was given the task of determining whether funding should be continued for a compensatory education program, he or she would want information on the following questions: (1) What was the basis of evaluating the compensatory education program? That is, were specific guidelines used, was a rationale for the guidelines put forth, and did the evaluator accomplish his goals? (2) If, in the evaluation process, specific instruments or tests were used, were these methods valid and reliable ways of measuring the outcomes of the program? (3) And, if the evaluation process generates empirical data, is this information the kind needed for the policy maker to make a rational and objective decision? These types of issues are dealt with in Part I.

In Chapter 1, Robert Ebel outlines some of the specific problems of evaluating educational programs. Ebel's basic contention is that evaluation programs have been abused in the past. He states the causes of these failures in terms of twelve basic reasons. Discussing first what an educational program is, he goes on to define "evaluation." He gives examples of evaluation and then examines the function of "outside" evaluators and some related problems such as the need for cooperation, communication, and the competence of the evaluators. Ebel goes on to say that one of the most important problems in the evaluation process is the definition of both the *means* and the *ends* of a particular program. He also emphasizes that the goals of a program need to be specified in the clearest terms possible; otherwise, it is difficult to determine if the goals have been achieved.

Ebel strongly believes that evaluation should be directed toward the end product of a program. If the quality of the end product is worthwhile, most likely the means used to achieve that product will be worthwhile. One of Ebel's concluding points, and an important one for the policy making process, is that the scientific method cannot always provide the kind of clear answers that the policy maker often desires. However, the scientific approach is still a vital component in the evaluation process in that it provides at least minimal guidelines for undertaking the evaluation.

In Chapter 2, Ralph Tyler looks at evaluation policies from the perspective of testing. Testing of various kinds is and probably will remain an important part of the evaluation process. Tyler is concerned with identifying those situations where the use of tests to evaluate may be appropriate, and those where it may be abused. While endorsing the value of tests in certain school situations, Tyler warns that abuses may set in when we try to make pupils fit the assumptions of the test. For instance, he argues that it is often dangerous to assume that student learning is distributed "normally." Tyler is also critical of the misuse of I.Q. tests; he contends that these types of tests seldom measure a child's capacity to learn. His criticism also extends to the heavy emphasis given to "scholastic aptitude" tests as the most valid and reliable indicators of successful college work.

Tyler distinguishes between *norm-reference* and *criterion-reference* tests and asserts that test makers should concern themselves more with criterion-reference tests, which measure the specific content that a learner is required to master. Such tests may range from a knowledge of how to add fractions to explaining the workings of a diesel engine.

What Tyler is basically arguing for is testing that is broadly based in terms of evaluating the learner on many dimensions. For the educational policy maker, the significance of Tyler's position lies in the range and quality of data that is provided for arriving at a decision.

In Chapter 3, which concludes this part, Steven Miller emphasizes some of the more general and conceptual problems associated with the policy making process. He points out first of all the logical problems encountered by the policy maker when he or she attempts to utilize research findings (the products of the instruments and tests described by Ebel and Tyler) in formulating and implementing policy. Secondly, Miller suggests that there are two fundamental problems in making policy. One is that there is no clear-cut consensus about what policy making is. That is, there are many and competing definitions of the term "policy" itself and that conceptual clarification is needed. The second problem concerns the belief of many policy makers that empirical research is always a "necessary" condition for formulating and implementing policy. In this regard, Miller points out that policy makers run certain risks when they use empirical research findings to make policy. Some of the risks include the use of inappropriate evidence and inadequate research designs and the difficulty of translating the technical findings of research into concrete decisions.

Miller's conclusion is that empirical research is probably not even a "necessary" condition in the policy making process. And he suggests that what is needed as a beginning step is a taxonomy that clarifies the levels of policy making and highlights how policy is finally derived.

1 Evaluating Educational Programs: Problems and Prospects

Robert L. Ebel

In recent years program evaluation has been generally accepted as an important aspect of the educational enterprise.[1] And a great many program evaluation projects have been undertaken. Some have been widely heralded and have resulted in noteworthy findings. But often the significance and dependability of the evaluative outcomes have fallen far short of the hopes and expectations of those who commissioned the studies and even of those who conducted them.[2] In this chapter we will consider some of the problems associated with program evaluation as it has been practiced in recent years. We will also consider what directions it might be useful for our evaluation efforts to take in future years. The discussion will be organized around twelve specific questions.

What Is an Educational Program?

A program is a set of procedures designed to accomplish a particular objective. This is clearly a very general concept. And one of the difficulties in discussing the evaluation of educational programs is the diversity of items included in that general category. Almost anything a school does can be called an educational program. Table 1-1 indicates something of the range and variety of such programs. All the various programs can be evaluated and need to be evaluated. The same general principles and procedures of evaluation apply to all, and the same general problems are likely to be encountered. However, the specific procedures that need to be followed in evaluating the different types of programs are likely to be quite different. And it will be helpful to limit this discussion by narrowing the focus to instructional programs alone.[3] It is these that have been the most frequent subjects of evaluation studies.

An instructional program does not encompass all of the elements that contribute to education. It does not include educational facilities, administrative procedures, characteristics of teachers, or qualities of students. It represents an important part, but only a part, of the total enterprise. Instructional programs themselves may be quite diverse. They may have goals as specific as "ability to add two common fractions" or as general as "liberal education." They may be conventional or innovative. They may be designed for infants or adults. They may be local, statewide, or national. The principal common element is *purposeful instruction.*

Table 1-1
An Outline of Types of Educational Programs

I. Instructional programs
  A. Focused on subjects (reading, arithmetic, literature, composition, history, physics, etc.)
  B. Focused on units of study (metric system, sentence diagraming, simultaneous linear equations, poetry, westward movement, etc.)
  C. Focused on teaching procedures (team teaching, mastery learning, programmed instruction, individually prescribed instruction, computer-assisted instruction, audio-tutorial instruction, open classroom, etc.)

II. School service programs (scheduling, counseling, marking and reporting, discipline, placement, follow-up, etc.)

III. Activity programs (athletics, music, dramatics, forensics, hobbies, etc.)

IV. Developmental programs (health education, career education, affective education, moral education, character education, religious education, etc.)

V. Problem oriented programs (compensatory education, special education, integration, dropout prevention, drug education, sex education, etc.)

VI. School operations programs (performance contracting, voucher system, in-service training, year-round school, community school, etc.)

What Is Meant by the Evaluation of an Instructional Program?

An *evaluation* is a judgment of merit or worth. It provides an answer to the question, How good? This distinguishes evaluation from *measurement*, which provides an answer to the question, How much? It also distinguishes evaluation from *assessment*, which is essentially descriptive. Assessments frequently include measurements along with other less quantitative descriptive information.

Evaluations always are, or should be, based on assessments. Sometimes they are based solely on the measurements provided by test scores. This is usually indefensible, for it can result in evaluations that are quite unfair. But even when based on comprehensive assessment data, evaluations may also be unfair. They require rational inferences and value judgments that can be highly subjective and personal. The best remedy for this is to use group deliberations in arriving at evaluative judgments. In general, the greater the number of competent evaluators who deliberate on the inferences and judgments, the sounder the evaluations are likely to be. Thus to make a sound evaluation of an instructional program is no simple matter. But this is not a valid reason for avoiding the task. Continuing failure to evaluate allows progressive deterioration of the program and offers no real incentive for significant efforts toward improvement. Consistent efforts to evaluate an instructional program, imperfect as they may be, are essential to the pursuit of excellence in education.

Perhaps a word should be said here about the relation of instructional *program* evaluation and *curriculum* evaluation. Strictly speaking the words "program," and "curriculum" have somewhat different meanings. However, as the terms have been used in most recent books and articles on evaluation, they refer to processes dealing with essentially the same materials and having essentially the same goals.[4] For purposes of this discussion, no significant distinction needs to be made between instructional program evaluation and curriculum evaluation.

What Are Some Examples of Program Evaluations?

To illustrate the nature and scope of program evaluation it will be helpful to briefly describe some efforts that have been made over the years:[5]

1. The Boston surveys in the 1840s, directed by Horace Mann and using common written examinations (instead of the conventional individual oral examination questions) to assess pupil achievements in Boston grammar and writing schools, intended as a basis for subsequent evaluation of their instructional programs.
2. Joseph M. Rice's use of spelling tests in the 1890s to indict the then current methods used to teach spelling and support his demands for reform.
3. The Pennsylvania study of pupil achievements in the 1920s, directed by Ben D. Wood and William S. Learned, intended to demonstrate shortcomings and to motivate efforts toward improvement.
4. The Eight Year Study, directed by Ralph W. Tyler, designed to evaluate the outcomes of programs of progressive education and to examine the impact of progressive education on subsequent success in college.
5. The National Assessment of Educational Progress, begun in the 1960s to provide data on educational achievements in various areas of learning by pupil groups of different ages from different environments, intended for use in evaluating educational accomplishments and needs.
6. The cross-national survey of achievements in mathematics, begun in the 1960s, to provide a basis for evaluating the effectiveness of mathematics learning in different countries.
7. An evaluation of the educational outcomes of Sesame Street, the television program for children.[6]
8. Evaluations of the outcomes of innovative curricula in physics, chemistry, biology, mathematics, and other subject areas during the last three decades.[7]
9. Innumerable local studies of programs in particular subject areas, specific courses, or units of study.

Is Outside, Independent Evaluation of an Instructional Program Desirable?

There are several reasons why outside specialists are sometimes employed to evaluate an instructional program. If the program development activity is being financed by a grant, the contract with the granting agency may specifically require external evaluation and provide funds for it. The independent evaluator is considered to be more objective and impartial than the project director or members of his staff might be. Had it not been for such externally financed educational development projects, it is unlikely that external program evaluation would ever have become a popular (and modestly profitable) enterprise. Another reason is that educators with creative program development ideas sometime feel that they lack instructional program evaluation skills. They therefore seek the help of outside evaluation specialists.

But external evaluations also involve problems. One is communication. The program developer and user must communicate to the evaluator the purpose of the program, the kind of evaluative information that is required or will be most useful, and the conditions that may facilitate or impede observations or data collection. The evaluator must communicate to the program developer, user, and other interested parties the results of his evaluation in terms that will be meaningful to them. Even in the best of circumstances, an external evaluator cannot be as fully aware of the program intent or design as the program developer. The evaluator cannot be acquainted as intimately with its successes and failures as those who work with it daily. Thus, there is a considerable price to be paid for the impartiality and expertness of the external evaluator.

Separation of evaluation from program development and operation creates another problem. Whereas the development and operation are more or less continuous, the evaluation is often confined to a relatively brief period in the life of the program. Its scope is thus limited and possibilities for constructive feedback are limited. If those directly involved in the program were skilled in evaluation techniques, and if they could be counted on to report with complete candor, they could probably produce a more valid program evaluation than an external evaluator is likely to do.

A third problem, which faces the external evaluator, is that of obtaining cooperation. Outside evaluations often generate anxieties with the program developers and users. Data collection can sometimes cause substantial interference with program operations. It is easy to understand why external evaluators sometimes encounter open or covert opposition; why they sometimes obtain less cooperation than they need to do their work easily or adequately.

On the other hand, if external evaluators are paid or otherwise rewarded by the program developer or user, and if they wish to continue that kind of employment, they are under some constraint to produce an evaluation that will be pleasing to those who are paying them. The evaluators' cooperation with their clients is likely to be excellent. The evaluators can be expected to look hard for favorable things to say about the program. When this occurs, the evaluation is no longer wholly independent or, indeed, external. Its validity is open to question.

Yet another problem with external evaluations concerns the competence of the evaluators. Quite naturally, external evaluators differ in the levels of skill they bring to the task. They differ also in the diligence and care with which they are inclined or feel obliged to work. Unless those who engaged the evaluation specialist are themselves competent evaluators (which is rarely the case), they may find it difficult to determine how well or badly they are being served. The evaluator, on the other hand, subject to no effective controls on the quality of his work, finds it quite easy to earn maximum fees with minimum effort, if he is so inclined.

Successful specialists in program evaluation tend to be agreeable men and women who are familiar enough with the language and basic procedures of evaluation to impress but not to overawe their employers. Only rarely are they experts in test development, survey research techniques, statistical analysis of data, or educational theory. They are likely to be well acquainted with various models or systems for evaluation, and to place more emphasis on how the evaluation task is to be approached than on how expertly it is done. As a result, educational administrators sometimes get less in the way of evaluation expertise than they need and think they are getting.

It seems probable that the importance of models and systems for instructional program evaluation has been exaggerated in recent years.[8] Some of them simply call attention to a number of fairly obvious variables that are likely to affect program results. Others present rather elaborate diagrams of sequences of operations that would probably be followed naturally, even in the absence of the diagram, by a reasonable evaluator. In most cases such models and systems have much to say about the form than about the substance of the evaluation. Often what they have to say even about the form of evaluation is not particularly enlightening. They place more emphasis on appropriateness in the selection of processes than on skill in carrying them out. Offering systems of quite general applicability, they give the evaluator little help in dealing with the variety of unique, specific problems that are likely to arise in practical evaluation situations. But models do serve some program evaluators well, enabling them to speak of their work in a special language that others only partly understand. This may confer on them a kind of expertise whose speciousness is not immediately obvious.

Thus, for a number of reasons, external evaluation is often far from an ideal solution to the program evaluation problem. It may sometimes be essential. It can sometimes be done very effectively. But for a majority of educational operations, internally generated instructional program evaluations and evaluation reports are likely to have a more constructive influence on the improvement of the educational product.

To make internal evaluation succeed at least three things are required. First, periodic evaluations of educational accomplishments need to be required by some education authority–local, state, or national. Second, a sample of the evaluation reports submitted by the local evaluator needs to be audited by the authority that requested them.[9] Third, local school personnel need to receive enough training in evaluation procedures so that they can do the job adequately. Practical evaluation techniques are not so highly technical nor so remote from typical school operations as to require development of a separate profession of instructional program evaluation. Anyone who is competent to design programs and to teach can also become competent to assess the results of teaching.

Emphasis on internal program evaluation should not be taken to mean that all tests and other devices used to supply assessment data for the evaluation should also be generated internally. Standardized tests, wide-scale testing programs, and other professionally developed scales can often provide vital assessment data. Local evaluators can make good use of this kind of specialized help. But the ultimate judgment of How good? can best be made by those most intimately acquainted with the program and most directly responsible for the decisions to start it, modify it, or abandon it.

Should the Evaluator Undertake To Judge the Objectives of a Program as Well as Its Success in Attaining those Objectives?

Different instructional programs in the same area of learning occasionally seek to attain the same ends by different means. But it is also quite common for innovative instructional programs to pursue different ends as well as to employ different means. The "new math," for example, did not try to help pupils do a better job of learning than what was taught in the "old math." Both the content and the process of instruction were different. Such differences in goals pose a problem for the evaluator.

Some recipes for the evaluation of an instructional program suggest that the first step is to determine the objectives of the program. The evaluation is then based on the extent to which those objectives have been achieved. This process of evaluation has the virtue of impersonal objectivity. But it runs the risk of ignoring the more important problem. If it does, it will have less influence than it should on the improvement of educational practice. If the programs differ in goals as well as means, as they often do, both goals and means need to be evaluated.

How Can Objectives Be Evaluated?

Objectives cannot usually be evaluated by the collection and analysis of data, though this may be what specialists in program evaluation are best qualified to do. It may often be the case that a person well qualified to evaluate the extent of goal attainment may be poorly qualified to evaluate the degree of goal appropriateness. But it will almost always be the case that both aspects require evaluation.

Essentially, the process involves inferences concerning the probable consequences of the pursuit of alternative goals and judgments of the value of those consequences. The better informed, the more rationally minded, the more willing to seek information and to spend time in reflective thought and discussion the goal evaluator is, the better his inferences and judgments are likely to be. Further, the consensus of a group of competent educators should yield judgments more valid than those of a single individual.

What Goals Are Appropriate?

Some educators complicate the task of goal evaluation by specifying goals that they have not defined clearly, and for which no practical programs of instruction and no reliable means of assessment have been developed. Such goals serve little, if any, useful purpose in education, although they may indicate high hopes and best intentions. Since the goals have not yet been attained by conventional programs of instruction, they may suggest that the proposer is a real educational innovator. Because the goals are going to be difficult to attain, they can be used to explain away the inevitable shortcomings in attainment. Thus, they do have some short-run, practical uses but are nonetheless essentially deceptive.

Those who insist that valid educational objectives must be operationally definable with respect to both instructional procedures and methods of assessment are sometimes accused of believing that "If it cannot be measured, it does not exist." But that is an overstatement. What they do believe is that if it cannot be measured, its importance cannot be demonstrated. That is, until someone develops some means for achieving the objective, and for knowing that it has been reached, no basis exists for a valid claim that the objective itself is important.

The degree of attainment of every important educational objective is measurable. To be important, it must make some discernible difference in the capabilities or other characteristics of the person who has attained it. If it does, the basis for measurement exists, for all that the basic processes of educational measurement require is the possibility of verifiable discernment of differences. If it does not, how can it be said to be important?

This point is often ignored or overlooked by those who persist in pursuing unmeasurable outcomes. They chase butterflies and neglect to cultivate the garden. Surely the acquisition and command of useful knowledge has been and should continue to be the principal focus of our educational efforts.[10] There is enough work to do in that fertile field to keep all educators productively employed for the foreseeable future. They should not waste their time and dissipate their energies on objectives they have no good means of reaching and no real way of assessing that they have been reached.

Should the Evaluator be Concerned with the Product or with the Process?

An instructional program is a productive undertaking. It is concerned with the development of knowledge, of abilities, and of other personal qualities. Hence, it seems obvious that the primary basis for evaluating the quality of an instructional program should be the quality of the product. Whatever the attractive characteristics of an instructional process may be, if it does not result in a quality product, it cannot be regarded as a useful process.

This kind of inference may be sound, but it is often overlooked and sometimes even denied. Too many of the discussions and debates over alternative instructional programs focus far more attention on the process than on the product. Clearly the process is important. It is the means to the desired end. Further, both student and teacher are legitimately concerned with how interesting, enjoyable, or satisfactory the process is to them, simply as a process to be experienced. But to the extent that an instructional program is a purposeful activity, and not simply an end in itself, it must be judged by what it produces.

It is quite true that a generally effective instructional program may prove to be ineffective in certain special circumstances, owing to improper handling of the program, inept or disinterested pupils, or other unfavorable circumstances. Specific failures do not demonstrate general ineffectiveness. But to show that the program can be effective in favorable circumstances, one must show that it yields a quality product in those circumstances.

Why do some educators place primary emphasis on process? A few of them may simply be seeking to avoid accountability for a product of questionable quality. More may be convinced that the product, though important, is intangible. This opinion involves, as has been pointed out, a logical or semantic confusion. To be important, it must make some discernible difference. If it does, it is not intangible. Still others may believe that the important product is ultimate behavior, which obviously cannot be observed immediately. But any instructional process that can be counted on to lead to an ultimately valuable product is likely also to produce some immediately discernible intermediate results.

Thus it is difficult to find justification for emphasis on process rather than product in evaluating an instructional program. It appears that the program evaluator should be primarily concerned with what the program produces. In program development, process is properly the focus of attention. But in program evaluation, it should be the product. We should be slow to accept claims for the advantages of some new instructional program on the grounds that it is a superior process. There ought always be some basis, empirical or logical, for believing that it will result in a superior product.

Can an Instructional Program be Evaluated?

To ask whether an instructional program can be evaluated may seem inane or pedantic in view of the examples just cited and of the current interest in the activity. For example, several organizations specializing in program evaluation have been established. Countless evaluation reports have been written and filed. A number of books and scores of articles on the subject have been published.[11] Surely the evaluation of instructional programs has received abundant attention in recent years. How do the results obtained compare with the efforts expended?

Some of the program evaluation studies have attracted widespread attention and brought forth favorable comment. Many of them have produced data that can provide part of the basis for a program evaluation. But seldom, if ever, does a program evaluation study give a clear, unequivocal answer to the question, How good is this instructional program? Yet it is precisely such an answer that educational leaders often hope or expect to get from such a study.

Can an instructional program be evaluated? Indeed it can. But not simply, or inexpensively, or with certain validity. Nor can the uncertainty be banished by employing a team of program evaluation specialists to do the job. They may be skilled in collecting and analyzing data, in drawing inferences, and summarizing findings. But whether a given program is worth continuing or whether one program is better than another must be decided by someone who is in a position to consider the total situation. In practice the decision always is made, not by an evaluation specialist, but by the educational administrator who must take responsibility for the decision.

Can Instructional Programs Be Evaluated Scientifically?

Those who undertake to evaluate instructional programs may be led astray if they try to follow too closely the model of the scientific research study.[12] An instructional program is not a stable, natural phenomenon with predetermined, unalterable functional relationships. An instructional program is a human artifact, highly complex, infinitely variable, and subject to constant change. It defies precise definition or accurate measurement. The outcome of a "precisely controlled scientific study" of an instructional program is almost certain to be either inconclusive or misleading.[13]

Scientific research intended to discover functional relations has been most successful in areas where the relevant variables are few in number, where they can be defined exactly and measured precisely, and where they are related to each other in ways that can be expressed in relatively simple mathematical formulas. What the program evaluator is looking for is functional relations between program characteristics and educational achievements. But in the educational enterprise, the variables are numerous, their relations are complex, and the variables are difficult to define or measure precisely.[14] Further, the variables of interest and the conditions that determine the relationships among them tend to be ephemeral. They are human constructs, not enduring facts of nature.

In the early decades of the scientific movement in education, with its stress on experimental research, a great many "method experiments" were designed and conducted. Those experiments involved controlled comparisons of alternative instructional programs and, thus, were essentially scientific program evaluation studies. More often than not, the findings were inconclusive, and the investigator would suggest that further study of the problem was needed. Even in the cases where significant superiority of one method or program over another could be shown, the investigator usually cautioned that similar results could only be expected in similar circumstances. And those circumstances almost always were somewhat unique. It is difficult to find in the research literature on education a teaching method or an instructional program whose general superiority over other methods or programs, in a variety of education situations, has been clearly established on the basis of experimental comparison.[15]

What is the alternative to scientific experimentation? It is the process man has used for ages to deal with all sorts of complex social issues and questions of procedure. Call it "judicious deliberation." Such an approach cannot claim the kind of objectivity, precision, or conclusiveness that attends scientific experimentation. But the approach seems to be much more comprehensive, much more flexible, and much better adapted to the pursuit of wisdom and virtue in human affairs. That its conclusions tend to be specific rather than generally valid, and ephemeral rather than enduring, is more the fault of the problems than of the method of dealing with them. Judicious deliberation appears to be indispensable in the evaluation of instructional programs.

Should Instructional Programs Be Evaluated as Separate Factors in the Total Educational Effort?

One of the ways in which life corrects errors in our intentions is to prevent us from succeeding with them. If most of our attempts to evaluate instructional programs separately have not been notably successful, it may be because we have been trying to do the wrong job.

Surely it must be true that the results of instructional efforts need to be assessed. But whose efforts? Those of students, teachers, program developers, administrators, policy makers, taxpayers, and all others involved directly or indirectly in the educational process. Educational development is a complex undertaking. It demands the cooperative efforts of many people. The question being raised here is this: Does it make sense to attempt to isolate the instructional program, one element of the undertaking, and focus attention on it and evaluate it separately from all the other interdependent elements of the total process? Would it not be better to evaluate the final product of the enterprise? Then, if the product seems not to be entirely satisfactory, the educator can proceed as do the responsible managers of most other complex enterprises. That is, using the processes of judicious deliberation, the educator would consider which aspects of the process might be strengthened or improved so that the final product would be better.

There are several reasons why overall assessment seems to be substantially better than single-variable assessment. First, overall assessment recognizes explicitly that the effectiveness of the whole enterprise is not determined solely, or even primarily, by the effectiveness of a single element. One of the undesirable consequences of emphasis on the instructional program is the impression that the manner of instruction is all that really matters in education; that the student can be considered to be a more or less passive recipient of the education. Indeed, we sometimes hear an instructional program referred to as a "delivery system."[16] This seems to suggest that "learning" properly packaged and set out at the doorstep of the student's mind, would be automatically taken in, assimilated, and made ready for use. Such a conception of the learning process seems quite unreal to those who have worked hard to acquire knowledge and develop understanding. To them the initiatives and efforts of the learner, and the competence and skills of the teacher, are also fundamental requirements for effective learning.

Second, overall assessment recognizes that instructional programs are not interchangeable, plug-in modules. They are related to and depend for their effectiveness on many other elements of the educational process. A program that works well in the hands of one teacher working with one group of pupils in one situation may work badly in the hands of other teachers working with other pupils in other situations. To focus separate attention on the instructional program may be to neglect crucial interactions between the program and other elements of the total educational process.

A third reason why separate evaluation of an instructional program is often unproductive is the indefiniteness, complexity, and variability of the program itself. Instructional programs are hard to define exactly. Some of them provide only general guidelines to the teacher and admit such variation from class to class. Even if procedures to be followed are specified in great detail, teachers may choose or be forced by circumstances to stress one area and skip another. When variations are great from one situation to another in the implementation of an instructional program, it is hard to know just what is being evaluated.

What Is the Alternative to Separate Evaluation of Instructional Programs?

Most educational institutions operate various instructional programs. And only a few are likely to require special program evaluation efforts during their developmental stages. Among these few are those that have been supported by grants from government agencies or foundations which require specific evaluations of results. A few others may involve radical innovations in instruction that call for radical innovations in evaluation. But for the vast majority of programs, a system of consistent, overall achievement monitoring is likely to provide a sounder, if less specific and direct, basis for program evaluation.

Consistent achievement monitoring means, essentially, the regular, systematic use of achievement tests and other valid procedures for assessing achievement.[17] The tests used are likely to be of two kinds: (1) those included in the school's program for testing outcomes in the principal areas of instruction; and (2) those developed or selected by teachers to measure achievement in their own courses or subjects of instruction. It is desirable, of course, for the tests to cover all objectives of instruction. However, failure to reach this ideal is not a fatal flaw. To assess attainment of some of the objectives is infinitely better than to assess none of them.

One advantage of overall achievement monitoring over separate program evaluation is that it assesses the product of the total enterprise. It is, after all, the product that should most interest and concern us. Consideration of the product avoids the almost impossible task of isolating the influence of the instructional program from all the other factors that influence achievement. It avoids the implication that the program is the principal determiner of achievement, regardless of pupil effort, teacher skills, or the general educational context.

Consistent overall achievement monitoring avoids the one-shot approach that has often characterized instructional program evaluation. Overall achievement monitoring should be a consistent, continuous program, rather than a special, ad hoc project. Many schools base the evaluation of their efforts on periodic assessments of achievement. Instructional programs change. So does the context in which they must operate. It is quite unlikely that a one-shot program evaluation study will yield conclusions that are generally or permanently valid.

Finally, achievement monitoring does not require, as does program evaluation, the experimental comparison of alternative programs or methods of instruction.[18] The difficulty of such comparisons is that factors other than the program which affect achievement must all be equalized or randomized across the two programs. If they cannot be equalized, which is often the case, and if the randomized factors have powerful influences on achievement, precise comparisons are practically impossible in any study of manageable size.

Consistent overall achievement monitoring does not, of course, indicate directly how good or bad a particular instructional program may be. This, as we have noted, is difficult if not impossible to do in most practical situations. What the monitoring does do is provide a basis for judging whether changes need to be made in the total educational enterprise or whether changes that were made have been beneficial or detrimental. It does not tell specifically what is wrong or how to correct it. But it can reveal whether particular answers to those questions have proved correct or not. The evidence may not be overwhelming or conclusive. But if gathered and used consistently, such information can help move an educational enterprise gradually along the path toward excellence.

Conclusion

It is unlikely that the somewhat skeptical and generally critical view of instructional program evaluation presented in this chapter will radically alter the views of its advocates and practitioners. Many of them will be familiar enough with the difficulties and shortcomings that have been pointed out. Some program evaluators may even accept the diagnoses of the causes of those problems that were suggested here. But they are nonetheless likely to say that there is nothing fundamentally wrong with their conception of instructional program evaluation, and that what we must do is to somehow overcome the difficulties and correct the shortcomings.

They may be right. Time will tell. If in ten years centers for instructional program evaluation still flourish, if professionally trained instructional program evaluators are still in demand, and if the principal emphasis in evaluation is still on programs for instruction rather than on achievement in learning, then program evaluation will have proved to be more than a temporary, fashionable solution to our persistent educational problems. My guess is that this will not happen; when the money runs out, enthusiasm for instructional program evaluation will wane. I hope it will be replaced by strong support for consistent monitoring of the total product of our educational efforts.

Notes

1. Ralph W. Tyler, ed., *Educational Evaluation: New Roles, New Means* (Chicago: National Society for the Study of Education, 1969); Daniel L. Stufflebeam et al., *Educational Evaluation and Decision Making* (Itasca, Illinois: F.E. Peacock, 1971).

2. Walter Williams and John Evans, "The Politics of Evaluation: The Case of Headstart," *Annals of the American Academy* 385 (1969): 118-182; Robert S. Weiss and Martin Rein, "The Evaluation of Broad Aim Programs: A Cautionary Case and a Moral," *Annals of the American Academy* 385 (1969): 267-274.

3. Lee J. Cronbach, "Course Improvement through Evaluation," *Teachers College Record* 64 (1963): 672-683.

4. David A. Payne, ed., *Curriculum Evaluation* (Lexington, Mass.: D.C. Heath, 1974).

5. Robert L. Ebel, *Essentials of Educational Measurement*, 2nd ed. (Englewood Cliffs, N.J.: Prentice-Hall, 1972).

6. Samuel Ball and G.N. Bogatz, *The First Year of Sesame Street: An Evaluation* (Princeton, N.J.: Educational Testing Service, 1970).

7. Hulda Grobman, "The Place of Evaluation in the Biological Sciences in Curriculum Study," *Journal of Educational Measurement* 3 (1966): 205-212.

8. Peter A. Taylor and Doris M. Cowley, eds., *Readings in Curriculum Evaluation* (Dubuque, Iowa: Wm. C. Brown, 1972), pp. 89-135.

9. Michael Scriven, "An Introduction to Meta-Evaluation," in *Readings in Curriculum Evaluation*, ed. Peter A. Taylor and Doris M. Cowley (Dubuque, Iowa: Wm. C. Brown, 1972), pp. 84-88.

10. Robert L. Ebel, "What Are Schools For?" *Phi Delta Kappan* 54 (1972): 3-7.

11. Ralph W. Tyler, Robert Gagné, and Michael Scriven, eds., *Perspectives in Curriculum Evaluation* (Chicago: Rand McNally, 1970); Blaine R. Worthen and James R. Saunders, *Educational Evaluation: Theory and Practice* (Worthington, Ohio: Charles A. Jones, 1973).

12. Daniel L. Stufflebeam, "The Use of Experimental Design in Educational Evaluation," *Journal of Educational Measurement* 8 (1971): 267-274.

13. Robert L. Ebel, "Some Limitations of Basic Research in Education," *Phi Delta Kappan* 49 (1967): 81-84.

14. J. Myron Atkin, "Research Styles in Science Education," *Journal of Research in Science Teaching* 5 (1968): 338-345.

15. Norman E. Wallen and Robert M.W. Travers, "Analysis and Investigation of Teaching Methods," in *Handbook of Research on Teaching*, ed. N.L. Gage (Chicago: Rand McNally, 1963), pp. 448-505.

16. Michigan Educational Assessment Program, *Objectives and Procedures* (Lansing, Michigan: Michigan Department of Education, 1974).

17. Warren G. Findley, ed., *The Impact and Improvement of School Testing Programs* (Chicago: National Society for the Study of Education, 1963).

18. David M. Shoemaker, "Evaluating the Effectiveness of Competing Instructional Programs," *Educational Research* 1 (1972): 5-8.

2 Uses and Abuses of Testing

Ralph W. Tyler

In 1949 social scientists, testifying at the hearings on the proposal to establish a National Science Foundation, pointed to psychological and educational testing as a major scientific contribution made by Americans. By 1975, a reaction against the use of such tests in schools, colleges, and employment offices was widespread. It was charged that certain desegregated schools had resegregated their classrooms by assigning pupils in terms of their test scores. It was claimed that a number of school systems used the results of the National Teacher Examinations to justify discrimination against teachers from minority groups. Many teachers believed, and many parents were told, that the educability of children was measured by psychological tests and that those with low scores would not be able to do well in school. Protests against such beliefs and supporting practices led a number of large school systems to discontinue the use of intelligence tests, and some eliminated citywide achievement testing.

As a further consequence of the growing belief that important educational decisions involved both abuses and uncritical uses of tests, the National Education Association adopted resolutions condemning some of the current testing practices and recommended that tests be used only when they helped the classroom teacher. The Committee on Resolutions of the American Association of School Administrators recommended the substitution of *criterion-referenced tests* for the *norm-referenced tests* that had long been the core of school testing programs. The U.S. Supreme Court ruled that tests used to select employees were discriminatory unless their content was directly related to the job for which employees were selected.

The shift in attitude toward testing is largely due to the growing recognition that many school policies and practices have involved improper uses of tests, inappropriate selection of them, and errors of interpretation. But what the public and many educators are not generally aware of is that such tests were originally constructed and developed for certain particular purposes. And over time they have been adopted and used for quite different purposes, some of which the tests cannot validly or effectively serve. Furthermore, in order to construct and develop a test, certain assumptions must be made to guide the work. The assumptions made in an earlier period are not acceptable today because of changes that have taken place in social and educational conditions. Such changes in purpose and assumptions and their implications for the uses of testing deserve careful review if the mistakes that have been made in the past are to be avoided.

Testing for Sorting: Norm-Referenced Tests

World War I saw the first successful use of psychological and educational tests, which led to their wide adoption by schools and other civilian institutions. The two million men drafted for military service presented the overwhelming problem of organizing and training a large number of persons who had had no previous military experience. Who were to be selected for officer training and who for the variety of technical tasks–construction battalions, signal corps, quartermaster corps, and the like? The psychological advisors developed the Army Alpha Test and other classification tests that provided the basis for selecting and classifying the large assortment of young men. After the war, group tests, both of intelligence and achievement, were constructed and developed for school use employing the same methodology that was formulated for the Alpha Test and other military classification tests.

The methodology was designed to sort those who took the tests along a continuum, that is, from those who make the highest score to those who make the lowest. Such an arrangement permits the identification of the position of any individual in terms of his standing in the total group; for example, one score is at the 98th percentile and another is at the bottom quarter. Furthermore, the arrangement enables identification of those who compose any desired fraction of the group; for example, those in the top quarter or those in the lowest third.

By administering the tests to a representative sample of a defined population, like children in the third grade in American schools, the continuum on which those tests are arranged can be read as the distribution of all American third graders. It is then possible to overcome the limitations in comparisons within an individual classroom, school, city or state by referring to a national norm.

Constructing a Norm-Referenced Test

One of the problems in constructing a sorting test is to devise questions that differentiate among those who take the test. A question that all or almost all persons answer correctly does not help to separate the high-scoring from the low-scoring ones. The same is true for a question that few can answer correctly. Those that help most to discriminate are questions that half of the persons answer correctly and half do not. For this reason questions are retained that are at about the 50th percentile in difficulty, while most of those that are in the lowest or highest third in difficulty are discarded. This procedure produces a test that sorts persons efficiently, but the test is no longer a representative sample of the content being tested. Items that most persons have learned are not well represented in the test, nor are items that few persons have learned. Scores on such tests do not show the extent to which students have learned what the schools seek to teach, although many laymen interpret the scores this way.

The early test constructors recognized that arranging a population along a continuum produced a rank-order scale but did not provide units of measurement that could be said to be equal along the total continuum. On a physical scale of weight, for example, pounds have the same value whether an object weighs 150 pounds or 200 pounds. But the difference in "weight" between the 50th and the 51st percentile is a fraction of a pound in a normal population, while the difference between the 98th and the 99th percentile is much more. In an effort to produce a scale that would have equal values along the total continuum, the constructors assumed for both psychological and educational tests that the distribution of the population on the behaviors tested is bell-shaped, the so-called normal distribution. In making this assumption, they were strongly influenced by Darwinian notions that the environment in a given locality is constant over a period and that human beings differ in their capacity to adapt themselves to that environment, with only the fittest surviving.

Whatever the characteristics of the physical environment may be, the social and psychological environment of modern man is not static. Social institutions, particularly schools, seek to aid children and youth to acquire behavior essential to survival. The ability to read, to drive a car, or to compute, for example, are human behaviors that are not normally distributed at the survival level. To produce a normal distribution that involves those behaviors, test items must be developed that are far more difficult or unusual than those that appraise typical reading comprehension, automobile driving, or arithmetic computation. The requirement that psychological and educational tests produce scores that give a normal distribution is a constraint that results in many test exercises that do not represent what most people are being taught. In contrast, a test for a driver's license, which does not assume a normal distribution, is based on a representative sample of situations in which automobile accidents are likely to occur. Pupil promotion policies and many teaching practices assume that student learning is normally distributed, an assumption no longer acceptable.

Intelligence Tests

Another Neo-Darwinian conception was that the limiting factors in education and in human success generally were the limitations of human capacity, especially the capacity to learn, which was called intelligence. John Dewey had a different view. In his experimental school at the University of Chicago, he found few limitations in the abilities of the students but many inadequacies in the learning experiences that traditional schools provided. More recently, neurologists have emphasized that the demand on the human nervous system to employ oral language is as great or greater than any of the neural requirements for the learning of what is taught in school. Except for brain-damaged children, the limitations to school learning appear to lie in the inappropriateness of the learning experiences provided, rather than in the capacity of the child to learn.

However, intelligence tests were developed when the opinion was widely held that failures in school and in life generally were partly, if not largely, due to lack of native intelligence, often defined as ability to learn. Since intelligence was viewed as an innate capacity, it could not be measured directly. Some indirect indicator was needed, and it seemed sensible to look for tasks that children encounter universally and have an equal opportunity to learn. If some children had learned them while others had not, the former, it was reasoned, were more intelligent. At that time the test developers did not realize the great variation in children's out-of-school environments and how that seriously limits the number of tasks children universally encounter outside of school. Nor did the developers understand the differential importance families and cultures attach to those tasks, which motivate some children to learn and not others.

Intelligence tests in common use were constructed by selecting exercises thought to be universally present in a child's experience. These included a large proportion of vocabulary questions and questions about physical and social relationships. The original selection of items was administered to a sample of the age group for which the tests were to be used. Exercises were retained that (1) differentiated among children, and (2) a larger fraction of older children answered correctly than younger ones. The tests were later refined to give preference to items on which the proportion of children receiving high marks in school who answered correctly was substantially greater than the proportion of children given low marks.

This procedure furnished a test that identifies children who have learned the tasks the test includes, tasks that are correlated with age and with marks that teachers commonly assign. It does not, however, indicate for many American children their capacity to learn. Kenneth Eells and Allison Davis have shown that the vocabulary of intelligence tests is the common vocabulary of middle-class Americans but not of most other classes or ethnic groups.[1] They have also shown that the motivation of children to do well on the test varies markedly among different groups. Furthermore, as was pointed out by Truman Kelly forty years ago, intelligence tests measure so much that is included in achievement tests that it is not statistically possible to distinguish intelligence scores from school achievement test scores.[2] Hence, to give an intelligence test to ascertain what students are capable of learning and then an achievement test to measure what they have learned is a logical absurdity. Rather, it should be assumed that all children not seriously brain-damaged are capable of learning what the school has to teach. The task of the school then is to find out better ways of helping those children who are having difficulty.

Scholastic Aptitude Tests

Another kind of sorting device is commonly called the "scholastic aptitude tests." Such tests were developed in the 1930s to help colleges select for admission candidates who came from a wide variety of schools having different curricula and different instructional practices. Prior to that time, the Ivy League colleges selected students who had followed courses of study outlined by committees of the College Entrance Examination Board and who passed examinations based on the syllabi for these courses. Most of the colleges outside the Ivy League admitted all applicants who had graduated from an accredited high school and had taken certain required courses there. Some of these colleges also required the applicant to have an average grade in high school courses of C or better.

The admission practices of the Ivy League institutions largely limited their freshmen enrollments to graduates of eastern preparatory schools, while the dependence of other colleges upon high school grades did not furnish a means for differentiating among schools with different school populations and correspondingly different grading standards. C.C. Brigham, of the College Board and the Eight-Year Study Evaluation Staff, had shown independently that tests of verbal facility and of skills in solving quantitative problems furnished predictors of college success that were as accurate as any of the other bases used in selection.[3] After World War II, the number of candidates taking the Scholastic Aptitude Tests of the College Board or the Tests of Educational Development of the American College Testing Program grew rapidly.

Scholastic aptitude tests are designed to predict the average grades in college that will be made by the high school senior (or junior) who takes the test. Such predictors are possible when the teaching and learning conditions and practices are relatively stable, which has been the case until recently. Teaching and learning in college has depended heavily on verbal facility and, to a lesser extent, on the mathematical knowledge and skills of the students. The successful habits developed in the secondary school were also useful in the college. Hence, scores on scholastic aptitude tests and average grades in college preparatory courses in high school were useful predictors of grades made in college.

Now, however, the situation is different. Colleges are becoming increasingly conscious that such test scores and grades reflect traditional practices and do not adequately indicate the learning potential of many students. Furthermore, the attack upon discriminatory practices affecting minority groups has resulted in a number of major colleges and universities establishing the policy of open admissions. But unless this is coupled with a reexamination of educational practices and the basic assumptions on which the college operates, the policy of open admissions may result only in failure of the student to gain an education after he has enrolled.

The prevailing curriculum and teaching practices have been developed by both trial and error and thoughtful design. They have, in the past, worked well with youth from middle-class homes that generally reflect the values, beliefs, habits, and practices of the dominant culture. But when a college seeks to educate a much wider range of young people, it finds that society is composed of a number of identifiably different groups with different values, habits, and practices. The stable working-class group, for example, views college education as furnishing entrance to well-paying, white-collar jobs which confer higher social status. Furthermore, most families from the working class are uncertain about whether their youth can succeed in college. Hence, students from such families are likely to need a curriculum clearly related to their occupational goals, and teaching practices that furnish continuing assurance that they are succeeding in the educational program. Some of them believe that the college program is only a set of hurdles they must jump to get certified for entrance to the kinds of jobs they want. They have not seen formal education as making a real contribution to their competence but only as furnishing a paper credential. They often do not expect the content of the curriculum to give them competence and may be satisfied to memorize what they hear and read without trying to understand its meaning to their lives and work. And other groups within society view formal education from their own particular perspectives.

Students now enrolling in post-high school institutions who were not largely represented in earlier periods have different values, expectations, and habits from those coming from the dominant middle class. They, too, encounter difficulties in typical college programs. The present scholastic aptitude tests help to identify youth who are different from those who have been succeeding in college, but the tests do not indicate the student's potential for learning in an institution that seeks to help its students learn.

If college practices are to be broadened to help a wider range of students get an education, so-called aptitude testing must become a device for assessing and reporting the variety of talents, interests, positive attitudes, and successful experiences that characterize the high school graduate. In effect, aptitude testing should seek to furnish a comprehensive inventory of the strengths and limitations, interests, and goals of each individual. With this information, the post-high school institution can make a wiser selection of students for that institution. And the faculty is provided with information that is more helpful for designing the curriculum and working out the teaching-learning procedures than information limited to the student's previous scholastic success and scores on tests designed to predict his grades in a traditional setting. With a student who has not found significant and relevant experiences in school, information about his out-of-school accomplishments in work, in community enterprises, in peer-group activities, and in the home are more likely to indicate strengths on which his educational program can be based than is furnished by scores on scholastic aptitude tests or high school grades.

Achievement Tests

Most achievement tests widely used in America are sorting tests, norm-referenced tests, and were constructed by the methodology and on the basis of the assumptions outlined earlier in this chapter. If the test were employed only for purposes of sorting, many of the sharp attacks upon them would not be justified. But in too many places they are used for purposes other than sorting and for which they are not appropriate.

At times achievement tests are used to find out the extent to which pupils in a certain school or classroom have learned what the school tries to teach. The kind of test used should consist of exercises (questions, problems, and the like) that comprise a representative sample of what the school teaches. The school can then infer from the performance of the children on the representative sample the extent to which they have learned. But a sorting test is not a representative sample; it is a sample of items that differentiate among children and does not include those things that most children are learning and those that most children have difficulty in learning.

Sometimes achievement tests are used to compare the average achievement of pupils in each grade in one city or state with that of other cities or states. Because an achievement test has been administered in different parts of the country and has national norms does not guarantee the appropriateness of the test for every school district in the nation. Not only do such tests comprise a biased sample of items (because it concentrates on those that differentiate among children) but it also cannot include a sample of items equally appropriate to every school because different schools deal with different topics, abilities, and skills in different grades.

Suppose common fractions are taught in the third grade in some schools, in the fourth grade in others, and in the fifth grade in still others. A standard test used in the fourth grade will have items that have not been taught to many of the children taking the test. The constructor of a national test then faces a dilemma in trying to construct an instrument that will furnish a proper comparison of arithmetic achievement in the fourth grade. Clearly, common fractions is an important part of arithmetic achievement and should be included in an achievement test, but at what grade level? Some test constructors put this topic in a third grade test, some in the fourth grade, and some in the fifth. Quite commonly they use the percent answering an item correctly as the basis for selecting the particular items to include. But the interpretation of the 50 percent level of difficulty is different under different circumstances. For students who have not been taught fractions, those who answer an item correctly have probably learned it outside of school. Thus it is an indication of the educative effect of the home and other nonschool experiences. For those who have been taught fractions in school, a correct answer is an indication of the school's educative effect.

To avoid this dilemma, or at least to reduce its seriousness, tests can be given at the times when most American schools have completed a major stage of instruction in some of the basic subjects. By the end of the primary grades, most schools have emphasized a number of similar, important objectives, even though their order of development or their placement in the several grades may have been different. The same is true by the end of the secondary grades. Hence, national achievement tests can be developed for educational objectives that are common to most, if not all, primary schools and administered at the end of the primary grades. The same thing is possible for secondary schools. Because of the diversity of secondary school curricula, national tests are probably appropriate only for certain commonly offered high school subjects or for certain widely accepted objectives that cut across the school subjects, like writing, career planning, and so forth.

Another inappropriate practice is the use of sorting tests to find out how much a child or a group of children have learned in a year, a semester, or some other limited unit of time. A test appropriate for this purpose should sample quite specifically the things being taught during this unit of time. But a typical achievement test has few items that represent what children are taught in a single semester or year, and it cannot give any dependable indication of progress in learning over the period.

One of the major misapprehensions in achievement testing arises from the use of the term "grade level" in reporting results of sorting tests. Such expressions as "this seventh grade is at the fourth grade level in science" or "this third grade child is at the fifth grade level in arithmetic" are often used. The first statement would imply that the seventh grade class has learned what science is taught in the fourth grade but not what is taught in the grades above the fourth. Actually, the test results showed that the mean score of that seventh grade on the science test was the same number as the 50th percentile of fourth grade children in the norm population. However, an examination of the test booklets reveals that the seventh graders answered correctly many of the items that are in the fifth and sixth grade course of study but few of those that are in the third and fourth grade. Therefore, having the same average score as the fourth grade norm does not mean that the students have learned what fourth graders have learned.

What is often overlooked is the fact that the norm scale is based on exercises that differentiate among children. They are not representative samples of each grade. Thus, the results cannot properly be interpreted in terms of grade levels.

Criterion-Referenced Tests

School personnel have increasingly become conscious of the inadequacies of norm-referenced sorting tests for some of the purposes they have been expected to serve. And attention is being given to criterion-referenced tests. But although this is a desirable development, two problems have already emerged. One is the frequent failure to define the particular criterion to which a test refers. The other is the mistake of carrying over methods of test construction and data analysis that have been developed for sorting tests and are not appropriate for criterion-referenced tests.

A criterion-referenced test of educational achievement is one that presents the student with a set of exercises that comprise a representative sample of certain things learned. The definition of these "certain things learned" is the criterion, which may be of different degrees of generality, complexity, and precision. The criterion may, for example, be "ability to comprehend the plain-sense meaning of typical news items in newspapers, instructions for assembling appliances, and instructions on income tax and social security forms"; "adding two fractions with denominators less than 10"; or "explaining the operation of a diesel engine in terms of physical principles." A criterion-referenced test cannot be spoken of generally. Rather, a test that is constructed to appraise the student's achievement of a specified criterion is meant.

If, for example, a test is to be used for appraising a new educational program designed to help disadvantaged children learn, the criterion will be relatively specific, focusing on small increments of learning that might be expected in a semester or a year. If, however, a test is to be used to monitor the continuing educational progress of a school system, the criterion will be more general. It will be specific enough to identify the location of major difficulties but not as specific as the classroom teacher might need. There must be general recognition by educators that criterion-referenced tests must be constructed and selected in terms of a clearly defined criterion appropriate for the use to which it is to be put. Otherwise serious errors will be made in the use of these tests, as have occurred in the use of sorting tests.

In the early years of the development of standardized achievement tests, criterion-referenced tests were developed along with norm-referenced ones. In 1893 J.M. Rice reported the results of a criterion-referenced test in his monumental monograph for the Committee on Economy of Time of the National Education Association entitled, "The Futility of the Spelling Grind." Freeman's Handwriting Scale, Gray's Oral Reading Test, and Hillega's Composition Scale are illustrations of standard criterion-referenced tests produced in the 1910s. These tests, however, were harder to construct and no more useful for sorting purposes than norm-referenced tests. Hence, the orthodox test doctrine, on which contemporary test makers have been nurtured, deals with norm-referenced tests. It will take time before sound procedures for criterion-referenced tests are in widespread use and a large variety of such tests are on the market.

Conclusion

Educators are currently questioning the uses of testing and are recognizing that serious abuses have developed since standard tests were first introduced in

American schools in the years following World War I. These abuses, however, are not inherent in all testing but have arisen from the failure to develop tests, testing procedures, and methods of analysis and interpretation appropriate to the changing conditions and purposes of American education.

The general meaning of the term "test" is indicated in the common expression, "Let us put this to a test." Opinions about what children are learning and how they are thinking, feeling, and acting, often lack an adequate basis in fact. To test an opinion is to obtain actual evidence regarding what is believed. That is the purpose of testing. In the broad sense, an educational test may involve not only questions to be answered and tasks to be performed but also observations of student behavior, appraisals of products made, interviews, and reviews of records made for other purposes. The development of tests and testing from this broad point of view is essential to formulating sound educational policies because unsupported opinions are too fallible to be defensible. We are on the threshold of a new development in testing and can be guided by an understanding of the errors of the past.

Notes

1. Kenneth W. Eells and Allison Davis, *Intelligence and Cultural Differences* (Chicago: University of Chicago Press, 1951).
2. Truman L. Kelly, *Crossroads in the Minds of Men* (Stanford, Calif.: Stanford University Press, 1935).
3. C.C. Brigham, *A Study of Error* (New York: College Entrance Examination Board, 1932); also see Wilford M. Aikin et al., *Story of the Eight-Year Study* (New York: Harper and Row, 1942).

3 Social Research and Educational Policy Making: Some Conceptual and Methodological Issues

Steven I. Miller

A great deal of literature has recently appeared on the relationship of empirical research to policy decisions. Much of it has centered around James Coleman's major work on the inequalities in educational opportunity in American education.[1] There is both support and criticism of Coleman's work, which has led to an examination of the entire issue of equality of educational opportunity in terms of two major areas: methodology and policy implications.

Glen Cain and Harold Watts, for example, have criticized Coleman's use of *regression analysis* insisting that the analysis was severely handicapped by lack of an adequate theoretical model.[2] Samuel Bowles and Henry Levine have likewise pointed out methodological problems connected with Coleman's Equality of Educational Opportunity Survey.[3] In response to these criticisms, Coleman has attempted to clarify his own reasons for choosing the particular methodology used in the report and the types of policy inferences that can be drawn from it.[4] Other writers, such as David Armor, while criticizing specific aspects of Coleman's findings, have tended in general to support them.[5] Coleman's report has served, then, as a springboard for the identification of two crucial areas: the methodological problems inherent in doing large-scale social research projects, and the effects that this type of research has on educational policy making.

Keeping those two perspectives in mind, the purpose of this chapter will be to (1) examine some of the logical problems involved in defining policy making, (2) examine the relationship of empirical research findings to policy making, and (3) suggest a typology that may clarify some of the conceptual and empirical difficulties associated with this area.

Research Findings and Policy

Much stress in the last few years has been placed on showing how empirical research findings can be utilized in making important policy recommendations for decision makers. There seems to be a growing consensus that the research establishment can provide certain vital information to those engaged in policy formulation and implementation. That is, many of those engaged in research have come to believe that important social problems can be ameliorated through social action based on empirical findings. John Gilbert and Frederick Mosteller argue, for example, that "to get better schooling for our children, we must find out how to strengthen our educational system. This will require study and especially, experimentation."[6] They go on to state that what is needed to solve some of the pressing educational problems are large-scale, controlled field experiments.

Henry Dyer outlines several research strategies that may be useful in approaching complicated educational problems.[7] He argues that measuring only one aspect of school outcomes, comparing schools that differ on this measure, and concluding that the lower performance schools must be somehow "equalized" to the higher performing schools is inadequate and misleading. What is needed, instead, is a rethinking of educational goals for different schools and more adequate empirical measures of those goals. Thus, two schools may differ on a test of reading ability, but the lower achieving school may be doing well, given its initial inputs, while the higher achieving school should be doing even better in terms of its initial inputs.

Two schools may have different but equally legitimate goals or ends. Policy recommendations, according to Dyer, should be directed toward recognizing that differences in schools do not necessarily imply judgments of good or bad. Empirical research is needed to recognize and measure those differences in educational goals. And having done so, policy recommendations can follow. It could be argued that empirical research will not yield solutions to complicated human problems. Although this may be true, it denies the important contributions empirical investigations have made in at least pointing out such things as the serious inequalities existing in American society.

Empirical findings do not at all times provide the type or quality of information from which policy decisions can be made. For educational policy makers, research findings do not always lend themselves to appropriate conditions for making policy. What the research establishment has been assuming is that research findings should at least serve as a "necessary" condition for policy formulation and implementation.[8] This assumption, while plausible, is misleading. It could also be argued that some types of research efforts could provide the "sufficient" conditions for policy implementation.[a] Yet, many research findings are not implemented or utilized. Or, if they are implemented, contradictory results at times occur. Armor, for example, has shown that the "integrationist model" has not produced the intended results in terms of busing but, rather, has resulted in the crystallization of other unexpected phenomena, such as "black power" identity *within* predominately white schools.[9]

Problem of Definition

The issue of whether research findings are necessary conditions for policy formulation centers around the notion of policy itself. The term "policy," is

[a]I am using the terms "necessary" and "sufficient" in their philosophical context as applied to social science reasoning [see Richard S. Rudner, *Philosophy of Social Science* (Englewood Cliffs, N.J.: Prentice-Hall, 1966), pp. 10-52].

largely ambiguous. It may imply a variety of meanings by itself. Other meanings may be suggested when policy is linked to the issues of empirical research findings. That connection, although unclear, is crucial because of the way educational policy makers have traditionally thought of relationship between the two. In the formal language of social science, this relationship can be described as an "if, then" proposition. Thus we have the proposition, "if policy, then research findings." This, of course, implies that "policy" is a sufficient condition for research findings and research findings are at least a necessary condition for policy.[10]

For those engaged in educational policy making, a central issue then becomes: Can we substantiate the validity of the conditional statement? If the answer is yes, then the policy maker has good grounds for formulating policy on the basis of empirical research. If the proposition "if policy, then research findings" is true, then those research enterprises that do not conform to the proposition are deficient in design or not broad enough in scope or both.[b] But if the conditional statement is false, then one can either abandon the idea of research influencing policy altogether or attempt to examine other factors that may be of influence. For example, it could be argued that policy is, in the final analysis, a matter of "political" concerns.

The position taken here is that the conditional statement under examination is true in a probabilistic sense (as are all conditional statements since they are confirmed inductively). That is, much educational policy is probably based on research findings, but it is not clear what the *process* is in determining the relationship between research findings and policy. For instance, under what conditions do findings become translated into policy? A beginning step in exploring the relationship between the two factors would be to concentrate on the *meaning* of policy. There is, of course, the important *normative* question of what "ought to be " the relationship of research and policy, but this is beyond the scope of this chapter.

The concept of policy is unclear as it is used in social science and educational literature. Does the concept have a roughly equivalent meaning in all contexts, or is it to be used selectively? Frederick Mosteller and Daniel Moynihan list seventeen references in their index bearing on the questions of educational policy, but seldom is the term "policy" defined explicitly.[11] Similarly, Cain and Watts, while placing heavy emphasis on the relationship of empirical research to policy, use the concept of a policy in different ways.[12] They also make reference to "non-policy" variables and "educational policy," and there is one reference in which policies they define as "specific activities." In Coleman's reply to the Cain and Watts article, there are, again, many references to "policy": "Policy advice," "policy-relevant results," and so forth.[13] Although

---

[b]I am assuming here, of course, that there has been at least an implicit commitment on the part of the researcher to see the research findings implemented, in at least a broad way, so as to have some influence on social problems or policy formulation or both. This, however, need not be the case. The findings may have some relevance for policy at a future time, or they may have no direct relevance, or they may contribute to theory building but not necessarily to policy formulation.

the *intent* of these differing uses of policy can be intuitively grasped within the context of a particular work, it is still necessary to define and operationalize the term if it is to be meaningfully related to a conditional statement.

One of the best analysis of the uses of empirical research to shape educational policy has been done by David Cohen and Michael Garet, who describe policy as follows: "a policy, then, might be described as a grand story: a large and loose set of ideas about how society works, why it goes wrong and how it can be set right."[14] They go on to say that there is a close relationship between empirical research and policy, but the acceptance of policy based on empirical research is most likely due to other factors such as "political judgments." Although Cohen and Garet are probably correct in their last assumption, their definition of policy is too broad. In working toward a definition, a good starting point is *Webster*'s: a definite course or method of action selected to guide and determine present and future decisions. Other definitions of policy may include some of the following:

1. A policy may be a set of rules or procedures that are associated with some phenomenon (*x*) and that do not present a problematic situation; for example, a policy that governs faculty tenure.

2. A policy may be a set of rules or procedures that have been used for some period but that are now being questioned.

3. A policy may be a form of decision to do something or proceed in some direction that is made by someone *before or after* evidence has been gathered.

4. A policy may be a decision by someone to begin to investigate a phenomenon (*x*) in a certain manner (*z*) with the purpose of confirming or disconfirming certain hypotheses (*y*).

5. A policy may be any given set of actions initiated by a person to realize a goal. (The actions may be a function of power, persuasion, expertise, charisma, or some combination of these factors.)

While many additional definitions of policy are of course possible, the point is that some basic work is needed in order to arrive at a working definition of the term.

Utility of Research Findings for Policy

It can be argued that even though the concept of policy may carry various meanings, research findings should at least be a necessary condition for policy. But that contention depends on the problem under consideration and on who is "making" the policy decisions. Those conducting empirical research would likely favor that argument; but they often have no voice in what policies are eventually carried out. And it is possible that "research ethnocentrism" exists among certain groups of researchers that has led to the belief of an intimate connection between research findings and policy that in fact does not exist.

Nevertheless, there is probably some justification for saying that the research enterprise does not give to the policy formulator or decision maker the type of data needed to actually implement policy. That is, research findings may be of limited use to policy makers. Let us examine this assumption.

One problem in terms of methodology and research findings for policy making is illustrated by Duncan and Hodge.[15] They are concerned with determining the relationship of educational level and occupational mobility, while considering the impact of such variables as socioeconomic status (SES) over time. Such data would be useful for policy formulation. Say, for example, the director of the admissions program at a university is interested in knowing how higher education influences social mobility. Perhaps he has some doubt about the commonly accepted idea that university education per se leads to higher levels of upward social mobility. Or he may be interested in knowing whether other factors such as family SES are important determinants of mobility.

Let us assume, more specifically, that the admissions officer is charged with implementing a policy to recruit more minority group students because the university administration believes that more education leads to upward social mobility, which leads to improved life-chances, and so forth. And let us further assume that he is to implement this policy (the implication here is that the "policy" is already in existence and that it now has to be put into action) based on Duncan and Hodge's study. The question now becomes, What is the relationship of the methodology and the research findings to the implementation of the policy? Several issues can be identified:

(1) Given the research findings, is the methodology necessary or sufficient or both? That is, before the policy can be carried out, the admissions officer will want to know if the statistical technique in the study is adequate for the problem under consideration. Otherwise, he will have to investigate other approaches more appropriate to his particular concern. If the admissions officer concludes that the Duncan and Hodge design is adequate, then he is committed to implementing the policy in accordance with the research findings.

(2) However, he may consider the statistical technique only as a necessary condition for successful policy implementation. That is, he considers the statistical approach as only one (although "necessary") way of looking at the problem. And the research findings, while empirically sound, are open to further analysis and interpretation.

(3) The admissions officer could accept the methodology but reject the findings, which is unlikely. However, it is still *possible* that he could select the approach, arguing that the general methodology was correct but that the study itself was carried out incorrectly. It would, however, be contradictory to say that he could accept the findings but rejected the methodology.

(4) He could reject both the methodology and the findings as not being relevant to his policy problem.

(5) He may not even understand the methodology.

There may also be a situation in which the policy formulator accepts both the methodological approach to a problem and the findings of the research and yet is not capable of formulating policy: (1) the findings may not be easily translatable into policy action; (2) it is not known how *much* research evidence is needed in order to carry out a policy; and (3) different research findings may present contradictory solutions for the same or a similar problem.

Translating Research into Policy

A major difficulty in attempting to delineate the various aspects of policy making is that empirical findings are often not easily translatable into concrete decisions for the policy maker. Duncan and Hodge conclude that "education was [is] becoming a more important determinant of occupational status, in terms of both its net influence apart from level of origin and its role as a variable intervening between origin and destination."[16] Given this, it would be difficult for the policy maker, the admissions officer in our example, to adapt this finding into concrete policy.[c]

Let us further assume that our policy maker now has additional information in the form of other studies that have some bearing on his problem. William Sewell and Michael Armor, for instance, conclude that a student's neighborhood context "adds little to the explained variance in college plans beyond that accounted for by sex, family, socioeconomic status, and intelligence."[17] This finding could be valuable in shedding new light on the once assumed strong relationship of educational aspirations and college plans. McDill, Rigsby, and Meyers have indicated that "the educational and social environment of the school does have a moderate effect on the academic behavior of students."[18] And in a related study the authors conclude that the social composition of the higher school may not be as strong an influence on academic behavior as some previous studies had indicated: "these findings indicate that contextual SES serves as an adequate indicator of a school's normative climate when the institution is at either the low or high end of the socioeconomic continuum. However, SES context is not an adequate indicator for schools which are in between these extreme positions."[19] And Sewell, in an important paper on the sources of inequality in higher education, using a complex multivariate analysis, charts the influence (in terms of percentages) of various SES variables on the attainment of higher education. He concludes that SES variables as they are mediated by other variables are a highly predictive indicator of access or lack of it to higher education.[20]

All those findings are based on sound research designs, and the conclusions

[c]It should be noted that the Duncan and Hodge study and the others to be cited are, in my opinion, well designed and executed research efforts. I am only trying to point out the difficulties that may be encountered by a policy maker in attempting to implement these findings.

are significant as they provide new insights on crucial educational problems. But there still exists the issue of whether such findings constitute even a necessary condition for policy making.

Use of Evidence

Given that our admissions officer accepts those research findings, he must then ask if they constitute sufficient evidence to implement the policy under consideration. Even though he believes that minority student recruitment is necessary for eventual occupational mobility, what type of evidence does he need and how "much" evidence is required before he implements the policy? The "evidence condition" may range on a continuum from "very little" to "substantial." This, of course, begs the question of the *quality* of the evidence that is considered for policy implementation.

Use of Different Research Findings

Policy making is also faced with the problems of different research findings. First, there is the problem of trying to implement policy based on research findings that are contradictory or at least seem to be. Second, there are research findings that have a certain credibility at one point in time but are subsequently shown to have certain inherent (usually methodological) weaknesses. Third, there are situations in which the policy maker is required to implement a difficult decision based on empirical evidence, but two or more opposing viewpoints are equally convincing. A case in point is the controversy over busing to achieve racial integration. For instance, both Armor and Pettigrew, in evaluating the evidence on busing, present convincing arguments–Armor against the policy and Pettigrew for it.[21] Fourth, there are cases where a policy is implemented, but a reanalysis of the evidence at some future time reveals that the evidence did not warrant the decision. For example, Miller and Kavanagh have shown that the empirical evidence on which the Supreme Court's famed *Brown* v. *Board of Education* decision rested was not adequate from a methodological point of view.[22]

Need for Conceptualization and Data on Policy Making

What this chapter has attempted to show is that empirical research is and will continue to be used as a basis for educational policy making. But, while we depend on research findings to provide guidelines for complex questions, we do not have a clear picture of the *process* of policy making. It could be said that policy is and will continue to be made with or without recourse to empirical research. But, although this is probably true, it does not resolve the issue of how policy is made in those cases where empirical evidence plays an integral part of the decision making process.

As a step toward unraveling these problems, a taxonomy of some of the categories involved in policy making would be helpful. Then, as a starting point for a more rigorous conceptualization and design, the categories could be cross-tabulated.[d] Table 3-1 outlines some of the categories and does not intend to be exhaustive. Nevertheless, the researcher examining the policy making process would want to examine some of the components of the categories listed.

A classification in terms of the amount or type of evidence or both the policy maker employs is another possible classification. A further approach might utilize a series of hypothetical policy questions to determine the process of decision making at different levels. Another useful classification might be one in which researchers themselves could be identified in reference to some policy

Table 3-1
Taxonomy of Categories Involved in Policy Making

I. Type of policy involved
   A. Implementation of existing rules
   B. Research conducted to provide new guidelines for traditional policies
   C. Research for solving specific problems

II. Level of decision making
   A. University
   B. Secondary and elementary school
   C. Government agency
   D. Specific bodies, committees, or other groups within the above institutions charged with policy formulation or implementation or both

III. Power and authority of the policy making body or individual policy maker
   A. Decision making lines of authority within the group
   B. Power and authority vis-à-vis other policy making groups (if any) within the organization
   C. Degree of responsibility for both formulating and implementing policy

IV. Level and type of training of policymakers

V. Use of outside "experts" for policy making
   A. Experts used for formulating or implementing policy or both
   B. Relationship of expert to policy making body
   C. Reliance on or preference for certain methodological approach or theoretical model

[d]For example, we might want to know how key educational policy makers, such as school superintendents, use empirical research in formulating or implementing policy.

questions. Here interest would be in ascertaining (1) the researcher's approach to the problem and (2) his recommendations on implementing policy.

While many complicated combinations of the categories are possible, until the issue of "policy" is clearly delineated, it will be impossible to speak of the benefits of research or make far reaching social action recommendations. Raymond Bauer has summarized where our understanding of policy formation stands: "we have accumulated experience of human history, many men who have mastered much skill and judgment, but we are merely beginning to systematize our comprehension of what the process of policy formation is about."[23]

Notes

1. James S. Coleman et al., *Equality of Educational Opportunity* (Washington, D.C.: U.S. Government Printing Office, 1966).

2. Glen G. Cain and Harold W. Watts, "Problems in Making Policy Inference from the Coleman Report," *American Sociological Review* 35 (1970): 228-242.

3. Samuel S. Bowles and Henry M. Levin, "The Determinants of Scholastic Achievement: An Appraisal of Some Recent Evidence," *Journal of Human Resources* 3 (1968): 3-29.

4. James S. Coleman, "Reply to Cain and Watts," *American Sociological Review* 35 (1970): 242-249; and idem., "The Evaluation of Equality of Educational Opportunity," in *On Equality of Educational Opportunity*, eds. F. Mosteller and D.P. Moynihan (New York: Vintage, 1972), pp. 146-167.

5. David J. Armor, "School and Family Effects on Black and White Achievement: A Re-examination," in *On Equality of Educational Opportunity*, eds. F. Mosteller and D.P. Moynihan (New York: Vintage, 1972), pp. 168-226.

6. John Gilbert and Frederick Mosteller, "The Urgent Need for Experimentation," in *On Equality of Educational Opportunity*, eds. F. Mosteller and D.P. Moynihan (New York: Vintage, 1972), pp. 371-385.

7. Henry S. Dyer, "Some Thoughts about Future Studies," in *On Equality of Educational Opportunity*, eds. F. Mosteller and D.P. Moynihan (New York: Vintage, 1972), pp. 384-418.

8. Stephen Cole, *The Sociological Method* (Chicago: Markham, 1971).

9. David J. Armor, "The Evidence on Busing," *Public Interest* 28 (1972): 90-116.

10. For an interesting discussion of the uses of symbolic logic as a tool for theory clarification and building, see Ronald Mavis, "The Logical Adequacy of Homans' Social Theory," *American Sociological Review* 35 (1970): 1069-1081.

11. Frederick Mosteller and Daniel P. Moynihan, "A Pathbreaking Report: Further Studies of the Coleman Report," in *On Equality of Educational Opportunity*, eds. F. Mosteller and D.P. Moynihan (New York: Vintage, 1972), pp. 3-35.

12. Cain and Watts, "Problems in Making Policy Inferences," pp. 229-231.

13. Coleman, "Reply to Cain and Watts," p. 349.

14. David K. Cohen and Michael S. Garet, "Reforming Educational Policy with Applied Research," *Harvard Educational Review* 45 (1975): 17-43.

15. Otis D. Duncan and Robert W. Hodge, "Educational and Occupational Mobility: A Regression Analysis," *American Journal of Sociology* 6 (1963): 629-644.

16. Duncan and Hodge, "Educational and Occupational Mobility," p. 644.

17. William H. Sewell and J. Michael Armor, "Neighborhood Context and College Plans," *American Sociological Review* 31 (1966): 159-168.

18. Edward L. McDill, Leo C. Rigsby, and Edmund D. Meyers, "Educational Climates of High Schools: Their Effects and Sources," *The American Journal of Sociology* 74 (1969): 567-586.

19. Edward L. McDill, Edmund D. Meyers, and Leo C. Rigsby, "Institutional Effects on the Academic Behavior of High School Students," *Sociology of Education* 40 (1967): 181-199.

20. William H. Sewell, "Inequality of Opportunity for Higher Education," *American Sociological Review* 36 (1971): 793-809.

21. David J. Armor, "The Evidence on Busing," *Public Interest* 28 (1972): 96-116; and Thomas F. Pettigrew et al., "Busing: A Review of the Evidence," *Public Interest* 30 (1973): 88-118.

22. Steven I. Miller and Jack Kavanagh, "Empirical Evidence," *Journal of Law and Education* 4 (1975): 159-171.

23. Raymond A. Bauer and Kenneth J. Gergan, eds., *The Study of Policy Formation* (New York: Free Press, 1968), p. 4.

Part II:
School Policies

School Policies

While Part I was concerned with some of the more general considerations of the role of evaluation in policy making, Part II deals with specific instances of policy as they relate to various educational settings. School policies involve the whole spectrum of decisions that in some way relate to the products, functions, and organizational patterns of schooling.

In Chapter 4, Virgil Clift deals with policy issues involved in structuring metropolitan schools. He believes that the present school-related policies as applied to urban areas are drastically inadequate. Although agreeing that schools cannot solve all societal ills, he feels that they have failed in even their minimal function—to teach basic skills. Clift suggests that any policies aimed at reorganizing metropolitan schools must be based on the following considerations: (1) closing the gap between what the community wants the school to do for its children and what the schools are presently accomplishing; (2) holding schools responsible for overcoming deficiencies related to deprivations owing to race, religion, or social class; (3) reorganizing schools to combat prejudice and racism; and (4) removing political considerations from the schools. Clift stresses the importance of reforming schools by emphasizing sound compensatory education programs. And he points out the need to proceed with desegregation efforts. He also sees the need for encouraging the development of administrative decentralization and community control.

For Clift, then, policies directed toward metropolitan schools should be both fundamental and broadly based. Only in this way will schooling "make a difference" for large groups of disadvantaged children.

While Clift's comments are directed toward reforming educational structures, implying that present structures are controlled by certain groups interested in status quo policies, Patricia Craig and James Guthrie, in Chapter 5, attempt to answer the question, "Who makes the important decisions about schools in your community?" In other words, who are the actual policy makers in public education? Craig and Guthrie begin by tracing the historical antecedents of control in American education. One of their main points is that school boards have become increasing powerful policy makers as a result of historically trying to separate the control of education from political machines and partisan party influences. The authors also document the interesting fact that school boards have gained increasing power as a result of school district consolidation coupled with a dramatic increase in the school population. These developments in turn have produced the "educational expert" today known as the "superintendent" of schools. However, Guthrie and Craig go on to point out that the control of education is still more complex because of the ambiguous nature of school districts as political units. Both local and state governments have overlapping interests, which presents further ambiguities in the determination of control.

In Chapter 6, Harry Miller looks at the relationship between teacher accountability and student achievement. There is increasing pressure by policy making bodies (such as school boards) to make teachers accountable in terms of their performance. This pressure is also spreading to various states and to teacher training institutions. At the heart of accountability policies, as Miller points out, is the belief that teachers are the key element in producing better student performance. Yet, what is really known about this process? Miller critically examines the most recent empirical research on teacher performance and concludes that, at best, we know very little about teacher characteristics, teaching styles, and school performance. He ends by saying that accountability will proceed as a key educational policy but one that is largely based on myth instead of reality.

For T.M. Stinnett and Raymond Cleveland, one of the crucial educational developments of recent years has been the growth of teacher organizations and their impact on shaping school policies. In Chapter 7, Stinnett and Cleveland emphasize that teacher organizations will increase in size and power and will become a major factor in determining a wide range of policy issues in the coming years. They caution, however, that this newly acquired power may be counterproductive if it goes against the public interest, serves as a base for the accumulation of personal power, and uses children as political pawns to gain more power. The authors then review historically the growth of the National Education Association and American Federation of Teachers. They contend that these two organizations may eventually battle for control, and the winner will represent the most powerful teacher organization in American education. The authors conclude that this will have large-scale implications for educational policy making.

Shifting the focus to higher education, Martin Haberman, in Chapter 8, discusses the policy of granting the "external degree," which he contends may have far reaching consequences. An external degree is one that "does not require residential study in a particular place." The idea is to give academic credit to persons in lieu of formal academic requirements.

Haberman reviews the pros and cons of restructuring higher education according to the life-experience criterion. While generally negative to the idea, Haberman points out that policy makers in higher education must decide whether to encourage this trend. The decision is difficult, however, because there are two competing alternatives: economically it may be a good policy to pursue, but politically it may result in a drastic alteration of the concept of the university. Haberman makes the point that at present the policy dilemma cannot be resolved because most policy makers are unwilling to gather the type of data necessary to evaluate the impact of such programs.

4 Organizing Metropolitan Schools

Virgil A. Clift

The public schools in the metropolitan areas of the United States are in serious trouble. And when the public schools are in trouble in a society that strives for democracy, that society is in trouble. Thomas Jefferson once said, "If a nation expects to be ignorant and free, it expects something that has never been and can never be." Almost 200 years later that statement still holds. There are too many young people from lower socioeconomic and minority groups in every major metropolitan area in America who are not being taught how to be responsible citizens in a democracy.

The nation is plagued with such compelling problems as inflation, recession, unemployment, underemployment, air pollution, contamination of the water supply, food and energy shortages. Cities are characterized by decay and crime, and institutions and government agencies are not responsive to the needs of individuals. National polls show that citizens have lost faith in their leaders and their institutions. There is little evidence that the leadership of the nation knows what to do; no one seems to have adequate answers.

The public schools are not responsible for all the social and economic ills, but they do have a role to play in preparing a citizenry to solve the problems that confront society. Lawrence Cremin, president of Teachers College, Columbia University, is correct in seeking a new understanding of "the relationship between education and social ideals to which we aspire. Any narrow definition of education that ignores the larger issues of society is just not sufficient."[1]

Traditionally the American public school has achieved the expected amount of success in teaching the fundamentals, or the three Rs. But the public school has never done as well as it should have in achieving the goals Horace Mann, John Dewey, Henry Bode, George Counts, William Childs, and other progressive educators sought: It has not discharged adequately its responsibility in preparing citizens for a democratic society. It has not imbued citizens with the ideals that are consistent with democracy. It has not prepared citizens to deal with the issues and problems that confront society.

And during the past decades the public schools in the largest metropolitan areas have even failed to teach the poor and the minorities the three Rs. The majority of such students do not read on an acceptable level and therefore do not achieve as much as they should in other subject areas. Not only are most of these students typically below national norms in academic achievement, they are not acquiring acceptable social skills. Even with the current emphasis on career education, there is little evidence that inner-city youth are developing saleable skills.

Out of this state of affairs have grown demands to reorganize the schools. Parents and educators have become so frustrated with the problems of deteriorating school systems that they seem willing to try any form of school organization that gives promise of improving the situation. Since 1954 public schools in the North and South have agonized over problems of desegregation and integration. Subsequent emphasis has been on compensatory education for the disadvantaged. And more recently large city school systems have been decentralized. At present there are efforts to achieve equality of educational opportunity through equity in financial support. (It is assumed that the more affluent school districts provide a higher quality of education because of their larger financial resources.)

Many of the ideas on school organization have merit. However, usually before the ideas are implemented and made operational, political considerations become apparent and sometimes replace educational goals. By the time political conflicts among various power brokers are resolved, educators and parents often have lost sight of the educational goals and proposed organizational reform strategies.

Guiding Principles

The organization of public schools should be based on sound educational principles. Brief statements about some of the most important follow:

1. The first and probably the most important principle was stated by John Dewey at the turn of the century: "What the best and wisest parent wants for his child, that must the community want for all children. Any other ideal for our schools is narrow and unlovely; acted upon, it will destroy democracy." When suburban schools are compared with those in the inner city, or when the resistance to desegregation and integration are noted, it becomes obvious that the American people have little concern for the relationship between schools and democracy.

2. The public schools have a responsibility to help students overcome the deficiencies, handicaps, and deprivation that are the result of a low socioeconomic environment and the negative conditions imposed by race, religion, or national origin. Social class and caste systems determine to a large extent the neighborhoods in which individuals reside, the kind and quality of schools they attend, and the job classifications in which they are employed. Most children from poor families and poor neighborhoods begin school unprepared to meet the demands of the curriculum. They need special help to overcome their handicaps. The same education for children who start school on an unequal basis produces

neither equality nor justice. Instead of blaming poor, uneducated parents for the inadequacies their children bring to school, educators should design programs that will help those students to overcome such cognitive and social deficiencies.

3. Since racism and prejudice are responsible for most of the problems associated with the poor quality of education in metropolitan schools, both policy and practice in school organizations should be void of racism and prejudice. But too often just the opposite is the case. Schools are organized in ways that permit citizens of the community to practice their prejudices on the lower socioeconomic and minority groups. For example, across the country citizens voice the view that they believe in integration but usually prefer to maintain the community school. They say they believe in integration, yet they do not think that busing should be used to achieve it. The reality is that they do not want their children to attend school with black students, especially if it means traveling into the inner city. Out of frustration, rejection, and other negative factors, some black parents and leaders now oppose integration. The old axiom among orthodox philosophers is still true: When the critical philosopher points his finger at reality, the orthodox philosopher studies the finger rather than reality.

4. Schools should be organized and operated in terms of sound educational principles rather than in terms of political considerations. Too many school decisions are made in response to pressure from community groups and politicians and for short-sighted economic considerations. Education is a serious business; it is big business. The quality of life in the future is dependent on the kind and quality of the education now being provided. Therefore, to operate schools in terms of expediency and political pressure and in response to certain special interest groups is to risk national hazards in the future.

Organizational Alternatives

Four organizational alternatives will be examined in the following discussion, not because they are the only possible alternatives, but because they have received greater support in a wide variety of areas. The four alternatives are: (a) compensatory education, (b) desegregation and integration, (c) administrative decentralization and community control, and (d) financing education.

Compensatory Education

For more than a decade compensatory education has received special attention in most large metropolitan areas. The programs of compensatory education were designed primarily for minorities and the poor, who were usually referred to as being culturally and educationally disadvantaged. Efforts to improve ghetto schools through compensatory education continue to persist because of the continuing opposition to school desegregation in white neighborhoods, the unfeasibility of desegregation from a demographic and fiscal point of view, and demands from minority groups for control over and improvement of their schools.

The educational literature during the past decade is replete with programs for overcoming educational deficiencies for the disadvantaged. Federal funds from Title I of Elementary and Secondary Education Act have supported a wide variety of programs for the disadvantaged. But the existing evidence indicates that "compensatory programs in schools isolated by race and social class have resulted in no substantial or lasting improvement in students' academic competence. Evaluations have been undertaken in a number of different school systems, on programs with different emphases, under varying conditions of expenditure for school improvement." Although there is a limited amount of data, which are far from perfect, the results are uniform and cannot be ignored. They suggest two fundamental problems. "First, compensatory programs misconceive the sources of academic failure, locating them exclusively in individual children's 'cultural deprivation.' Second, there has not been a clear definition of 'compensation' nor of the required changes in the schools' programs and the magnitude of the effort involved."[2]

The disadvantaged in the caste system, typically blacks, Chicanos, American Indians, and most persons at the lower end of the socioeconomic scale, generally achieve from one to three grade levels below middle-class students by the time they reach the twelfth grade. The Coleman study[3] and others show that the social class and racial composition of schools relate to academic achievement. Poor children who attended school with students from the majority who were from affluent homes, performed higher academically than poor children who attended school with students from the majority who were from poor backgrounds. This has particular implications for black children and can therefore be used as a compelling argument for school integration.[4] Efforts to integrate schools should not be relinquished because that gives greater promise of solving the educational problems of the poor and minorities than does compensatory education.

But, since racism will undoubtedly be with us for some time to come, compensatory education will be useful to salvage minority children who are now attending school in an unfavorable situation. Therefore some of the fundamentals that must be followed in compensatory programs follow:

1. Probably the most important single feature of compensatory education has to do with developing positive self-esteem. Students need to feel that they are of worth, that they belong, and that they can achieve. Deeply ingrained negative self-images characterize children who have grown up in poverty and in a social environment of despair. Mental health and personality problems grow out of a

feeling of rejection and an inhospitable environment, which cause the child to feel that he is "nobody" and of little worth. These complex problems must be dealt with in order to enable the student to muster his personal resources for academic work.

2. The number of students per teacher must be reduced drastically. Class size should be small enough so that the teacher can perform both a tutorial and counseling function in addition to the teaching function. Classes must be small enough to enable teachers to give individualized attention on both personal and academic matters. The goal should be to help students to realize achievement and progress, to help them acquire a sense of belonging and personal worth, and to help them to gain an understanding of and an appreciation for education as a means of improving their stations in life and the quality of their lives.

3. Teachers should be selected who have a strong desire to work with disadvantaged minorities and who have been appropriately trained for the task. Parents and children in ghetto schools are firmly convinced that a large majority of the teachers in their schools are prejudiced. Much evidence indicates that teachers are not able to teach ghetto children. Many ghetto individuals who were failures in school have later been sent to prison where they become noted authors, artists, musicians, actors, and so on. Why have prisons been more successful than schools in such cases?

4. Some of the blame for low academic achievement and the failure of students must be shifted from the student and his parents to the schools and society. This society is unfair, unjust, and undemocratic in a variety of ways that have negative influences on poor and minority children every day of their lives. The inequities in housing, employment, and education, for example, are easy to document.

5. Ways must be found to obtain the support and interest of the parents. Parents in the slum areas of American cities are interested in and do support some institutions and organizations. Poor parents can be helped to become involved in and supportive of their schools. If teachers and administrators do not know how to get them interested and involved, they can gain insights from other community organizations that are successful.

6. Classroom discipline must be expected and required. No society can expect to remain civilized and free if public schools are permitted to operate with little regard for discipline and order. In far too many inner-city schools the children do not respect each other; they do not obey and respect teachers and administrators. In some schools policemen are stationed in hallways and yards.

7. Acceptable academic achievement must be expected and demanded. Regular class attendance must be expected and demanded too. The schools must prepare young people to be responsible, productive citizens who have a contribution to make to society. Schools cannot possibly accomplish this if they offer a watered down curriculum with low standards.

Desegregation and Integration

The cultural, social, and economic problems that grow out of the way American society is organized can be solved, in part, by desegregation and integration.[a] Much of the current thinking about the problems of desegregation and integration in urban areas has been focused on the black child. Thus, the objections to integration are based on race. On the other hand, the authorities in the behavioral sciences are agreed that cultural deprivation is not race-related. The ego development of individuals in each subculture is directly influenced by the special nature and quality of multidimensional cultural factors that are operating in the environment. Therefore, cultural deprivation is related, not specifically to racial factors, but to environmental factors: David and Pearl Ausubel sum up this position:

> Many of the ecological features of the segregated Negro subculture impinge on personality development in early childhood are not specific to Negroes as such, but are characteristic of most lower-class populations. This fact is not widely appreciated by white Americans and hence contributes to much anti-Negro sentiment: many characteristic facets of the Negro's value system and behavior pattern are falsely attributed to his racial membership, whereas they really reflect his predominant membership in the lower social class.[5]

Some of the cultural factors which will be described below contribute to deprivation that manifests itself in low levels of motivation; low achievement on standardized tests; negative self-evaluation; and low levels of aspiration and behavior that deviate from accepted middle-class norms. Probably the most promising way of dealing with these problems is through true integration. The urban population has grown and is growing increasingly homogeneous. Both the inner city and the suburbs have become a series of "one-social-class" neighborhoods. That is, people in a neighborhood tend to be similar in income level; general employment classification; amount of schooling completed; racial identity; and ethnic background.

The black migrant to the urban areas of the North usually lives in the worst and most crowded slum areas that are typically inhabited by his group. His economic resources, level of culture, sophistication, and style of living all operate to force him to seek the ghetto as a place to live. Once there he becomes even more isolated from the mainstream of American life than he was before moving to the city. His neighborhood, like the other one-social-class neighborhoods, tends to be self-contained and an island unto itself. It is in this environment that children begin to take on a value system and patterns of behavior that are inconsistent with the demands and requirements for academic

[a]"Desegregation" refers to racially mixed schools and the elimination of racial imbalance. "Integrated" schools are racially mixed; have desegregated classrooms; and have programs designed to reduce racial tension, overcome deprivation, and cause students to feel that they are accepted.

success in schools. Typically the neighborhood is more segregated racially than two or three decades ago as illustrated in Table 4-1, and the local school has ceased to represent a cross-section of American life. The population in the school is homogeneous. Therefore, the school provides little opportunity for cross-fertilization of ideas and cultures. It provides little opportunity for young people of different backgrounds to learn anything about each other. It provides few first-hand experiences from which children learn to build understandings of and appreciations for people who are different.

The school has become the dominant institution in the control and socialization of youth because it is a major force in determining their status transition. The child who is at the bottom of the socioeconomic scale is isolated from successful examples and models in the community and from schools that can be emulated. Examples of success and of behavior that lead to high-level attainment in the broader society are not a part of his environment at all. His world is void of abstract symbols, of ideas, of abstractions and of a high level of verbal meanings. Therefore it is not surprising that he has difficulty in making high scores on standardized intelligence and achievement tests.

The school tends to reflect the neighborhood in which it is located. Thus schools in the higher socioeconomic neighborhoods tend to be the "silk stocking" type, with better buildings and facilities, better and more enriched programs, and better qualified teachers. At the bottom of the scale are found the all-black schools in the all-black residential areas of the inner city. These schools are nearly always inferior in quality. The larger society usually regards the people who attend such schools as being inferior and assigns to them a stigma and a negative evaluation. The teachers, the community, and the board in charge of operating the schools do not expect anything but low-level performance. The curriculum is therefore accommodating and geared to a low level of ability and to shoddy academic performance. Consequently retardation begins for a large number of the children very soon after they enter school. By the time they reach the fourth grade, they are performing one grade below their grade level. The longer they remain in the school, the farther behind they fall. It is a combination of these and other social and economic factors (the most important of which is the enforcement of a negative self-evaluation on the black child) that disarms him psychologically. This author holds that the best and most effective ways of solving these problems are through an integrated society and integrated schools.

The data from Equality of Educational Opportunity Survey show that black students who attended school with whites for most of their elementary school career exhibited, on the average, about half the academic disadvantages of those blacks who attended school only with blacks.[6] In addition, studies of elementary school desegregation in a number of cities show higher achievement gains for black children placed in predominantly white schools than for black children remaining in predominantly black schools.

Although it might be possible to improve the inner-city schools by offering

Table 4-1
Percent of Black Students Attending Schools 80 Percent or More Black in Thirty-four Big City School Districts with One Third or More Black Enrollment, 1968 and 1971[a]

District	1968	1971
Washington, D.C.	96.5	97.6
Compton, Calif.		97.8
Atlanta, Ga.	91.8	85.9
Newark, N.J.	88.4	91.3
Orleans Parish, La.	83.3	80.8
Richmond, Va.	88.6	36.5
Baltimore, Md.	83.8	84.1
St. Louis, Mo.	89.0	89.8
Gary, Ind.	90.7	95.7
Detroit, Mich.	79.1	78.6
Philadelphia, Pa.	76.9	80.2[b]
Oakland, Calif.	77.1	73.1
Cleveland, Ohio	90.8	91.3
Birmingham, Ala.	92.7	74.7
Chicago, Ill.	90.3	91.6
Memphis, Tenn.	95.4	89.2
Kansas City, Mo.	78.1	86.4
Caddo Parish, La.	97.4	66.6
Louisville, Ky.	64.9	82.3
Chatham County, Ga.	86.5	7.6
Charleston County, S.C.	84.2	62.4
Norfolk, Va.	82.3	1.2
Cincinnati, Ohio	50.9	54.9
Mobile County, Ala.	87.5	44.2
Dayton, Ohio	82.7	78.1
Pittsburgh, Pa.	60.0	61.6
Flint, Mich.	42.4	46.6
Buffalo, N.Y.	65.1	59.0
Baton Rouge Parish, La.	94.2	72.0
Houston, Tex.	90.9	86.0
Indianapolis, Ind.	62.5	60.1
Dallas, Tex.	93.0	83.4
Rochester, N.Y.	34.4	33.7
New York, N.Y.	60.5	69.2

[a]Ranked according to 1971 black percentage in enrollment.

[b]1970 figure.

Source: U.S. Senate Select Committee on Equal Educational Opportunity, *Toward Equal Educational Opportunity* (Washington, D.C.: U.S. Government Printing Office, 1972), pp. 116-117.

compensatory education, and although many black leaders now advocate improving black schools by hiring more black teachers and administrators, the research suggests that integration is a much more viable and promising concept. Integration has greater promise of improving academic achievement for black children. It contributes to more positive interracial attitudes and behavior. It will help black students to overcome the negative influences of low self-esteem and the psychological damage growing out of the ghetto environment.[7] And, finally, integration is the only policy that "will make it politically feasible for the destinies of America's two separate nations to become bound up together. A policy of segregated compensation cannot provide that binding tie and, therefore, can promise only the continuance of a segregated, closed, and inferior system of education for Negro Americans."[8]

Administrative Decentralization and Community Control

American public schools have historically been under the control of local communities. But as the cities changed demographically during the mid-twentieth century, school administration became large, bureaucratic, and insensitive to the special needs and problems of children from a wide variety of backgrounds. In fact, it became obvious in the 1960s that schools in the inner cities were not serving adequately the students of low socioeconomic and minority status. One of the proposals to correct this situation has been administrative decentralization.

Since the 1960s many large school systems have been divided into smaller districts that paralleled the various communities. The major purpose of school decentralization was to make the schools more responsive to the needs of the children and the desires of the parents. Some local leaders, however, have voiced the opinion that the central boards wanted decentralization in order that some of the caustic criticism of the ineffective schools could be shifted from the central boards to the local leadership. Central school boards, especially those in the cities, had been bombarded by criticisms from local groups. With decentralization, the critical groups have had an opportunity to support candidates from the local level who reflected more consistently their views and desires.

According to surveys reported by Allan Ornstein and others, the major purposes for administrative decentralization are:

1. To reduce the administrative span of control.
2. To provide greater staff sensitivity to local populations.
3. To enhance school-community relations.
4. To provide greater articulation and continuity in the K-12 programs.
5. To provide more efficient maintenance and supply support of the school unit.
6. To reduce bureaucratic overlap and waste.[9]

Since 1967 most large- and medium-sized metropolitan school systems have been decentralized. Administrative decentralization follows a variety of patterns. In some systems only the high schools are decentralized and in others, only the junior high schools and their feeding elementary schools. There are, of course, other varieties of decentralization. The most frequent number of students per decentralization unit was found to be between 15,000 and 25,000 students.[10] New York City and Detroit differ from other large school systems in that administrative decentralization provides for community control with the elected school boards functioning in conjunction with the central school board.

The racial issue in metropolitan areas has been the most important force in community control. Many black leaders, often with the support of whites, fought for decentralization and community control because of the belief that only through these measures could blacks control the educational destinies of their youth.

By 1975 the political power of blacks was responsible for the election of over 3,000 black elected officials, which included over 120 black mayors, 17 U.S. congressmen, and 1 U.S. senator, 2 lieutenant governors, and over 1,000 local board members.[11] In the largest cities, where black elected officials supposedly exercised considerable power over school policy, there was no evidence that the quality of public education had improved. Mel Ravitz has accurately observed that, "the issue of black control over the public school system in America's central cities is fast disappearing as a pertinent issue."[12] The reality is that there is such an urgent need for radical structural change in the educational establishment that local control will make little or no difference in the quality of education, regardless of the race or color of those in control of local school districts.

New York City and Detroit best represent attempts to implement the concept of community control. In both cities political battles have raged over issues that frequently did not relate to the improvement of schools. On occasions those elected to community boards were not well enough informed to function effectively and efficiently on the boards to which they had been elected. Frequently also local school board members sought personal gains by being members of school boards. They sought to influence the employment of friends and relatives in various capacities in the schools.

In New York City another problem growing out of decentralization related to the fact that many teachers and the teachers' unions have often condemned the concept of decentralization and community control. Unions have resisted the idea of having personnel powers shifted from the central board of education to community school boards. Unions had won in their contract agreements the right to participate in decision making and school policy, and they were not willing to relinquish those rights to community boards. In the Bundy Report on decentralization of New York City schools, which outlined a program of community control of the schools, considerable attention was given to the power of the local boards to fire and hire personnel. The panel members felt that the local districts should have the power to recruit teachers and to dismiss them under certain conditions. Confrontation and conflicts emerging from these principles and issues have often become more important than the quality of education in schools.

In spite of problems and mistakes that have characterized community control, it is a concept with considerable merit. Local citizens may not know what quality education consists of and how to achieve it. Yet, they should be given a chance to hire administrators and teachers who are willing to try new ideas in teaching, administration, and the involvement of community persons in the educative process. If community districts were given wide latitude to experiment, it might be possible for successes in certain local districts to be replicated in others. Further, community control and wider community participation will have considerable value to the citizenry in the local community. It will help to remove their feeling of isolation and alienation. Wider participation in determining the educational destinies of children will likely lead to a better understanding of the nature of administrative structures in society and of how to make them more responsive to and effective in serving the needs of individuals and groups.

Financial Support for Schools

One of the most compelling problems confronting American society is providing equal financing for urban school children. Residential segregation by class and race has created an undue hardship on cities to generate adequate resources from their tax structure to provide quality education and other social services for inner-city children. Their counterparts in suburban districts, however, enjoy quality education at a lower tax rate. One of the basic requirements for entrance into the mainstream of America is high-quality education. It is therefore crucial that poor and minority children receive both an equal and a quality education if they are to compete on a fair and equal basis with others for available economic and educational opportunities. Several years ago John and Evelyn Dewey cautioned: "It is fatal for a democracy to permit the formation of fixed classes. Differences of wealth, the existence of large masses of unskilled laborers, contempt for work with the hands, inability to secure the training which enables one to forge ahead in life, all operate to produce classes, and to widen the gulf between them."[13]

There are several factors that have affected the tax situation in large cities. Schools are largely dependent on an archaic system of property taxation. The property base has become inadequate because urban decay has diminished property values in some areas. Many business and industrial establishments have moved from the cities. Freeways, universities, and public buildings have removed property that at one time was a part of the tax base. The middle class has fled from the cities to the suburbs taking their tax dollars with them. Low-income groups, by contrast, have remained; they possess little or no taxable income. What is also significant is that suburban dwellers obtain the high-income jobs in cities, with low-income groups mainly trapped in the low-paying service occupations. Although state governments do provide financial revenue to local school districts, it thus far has been inadequate to meet the needs of cities. Since many state legislatures are dominated by suburban and rural interests, legislators are more responsive to those needs and demands, thereby subordinating the problems of the cities.

It is not surprising that the present archaic, inadequate, and unequal tax system for financing schools is under attack. For example, in 1971 the California Supreme Court in *Serrano* v. *Priest*, ruled that education is a "fundamental interest" and thus cannot be based on wealth.[14] Poor districts were found having to levy twice the tax rate to support only half of the needed educational programs. Affluent districts, however, were providing a higher quality of education for their children while paying lower taxes.[15] The implication of the California decision was clear: Ways must be found to provide a more equitable financial base for education. Two years later in *Rodriguez* v. *San Antonio Independent School District*, the state's school financing laws were challenged.[16] Although the district court ruled in Rodriguez's favor, the U.S. Supreme Court later declared that education is not "a fundamental right" warranting constitution protection. Instead the Court took the position that education and state taxation are functions reserved for state government and its legislative processes.

While the Supreme Court has preempted the Equal Protection Clause of the Fourteenth Amendment as a means to void financing education through property tax, a redress of the grievance is finding positive results in the state supreme courts. In April 1973, for example, the New Jersey Supreme Court declared unconstitutional the state's traditional system of heavy reliance on property taxes as a means of financing public schools because the system had created wide disparities in the quality of education between wealthy and poor communities. The Court gave the state legislature eighteen months to approve a new system of financing schools that would presumably replace local property taxes. The legislature failed to meet the Court's deadline, and the governor filed a brief with the court asking for a drastic reallocation of state school aid. The proposal would withhold state aid from wealthy communities and divert it to poor rural and inner-city school districts. Table 4-2 points up educational inequities in New Jersey for the year 1974. Expenditures per pupil in the three highest districts ranged from $2,295 to $2,533; whereas, the range in the three lowest districts was from $942 to $962.

In December 1974 the Connecticut Supreme Court declared the system of school financing unconstitutional. The system, like that in other states, relied

Table 4-2
New Jersey's Educational Inequities, 1974
(Expenditures per pupil)

Three Highest Districts		Three Lowest Districts	
Union Township	$2,533	Fairfield Township	$942
Lower Alloways Creek	$2,440	Abescon City	$951
Englewood Cliffs	$2,295	Elmer Borough	$962

Source: Unpublished data from the New Jersey Education Department, 1975.

primarily on local taxes and was inequitable because wealthy districts provided more financial aid than the poor districts. The legislative commission in 1975 asked the state aid be increased by $10 million and by larger amounts each year until 1980. All new state aid was to be given to the poorer districts to bring their expenditures to within 75 percent of those of the wealthiest districts. These and other rulings mandate long overdue reforms in financing education.

In the spirit of New Jersey and Connecticut, several civil rights organizations are preparing an onslaught on the inequities in financial support in other parts of the nation. And it is expected that this will become one of the burning issues in education during the remainder of the 1970s. Many educators and legal authorities have also sponsored the idea that an educational amendment to the constitution has become essential to remove financial inequity. Now is the time to create and sponsor a national standard of education, if all groups in society are to reap the benefits of its resources. The time has clearly come to do more than document the dollar disparities spent on education in various school districts. New revenue systems are needed to generate and distribute school funds. Since the U.S. Supreme Court in *Rodriquez* shifted the issues to the state courts, they may be expected to play a role in reform. As Joel Burke has observed, "what has now become clear is that the courts have provided only an opportunity, not an answer; a starting point for reform, not a solution to the unfairness and irrationality of educational funding in America."[17] He goes on to emphasize the importance of the legislative process in contributing to meaningful change.

During this period of economic crisis for most cities, it is hoped that economic reform will also focus attention on the accomplishments of the educational system, since there is little substantiation for the position that educational need can be defined in terms of economic resources alone. Also, since there is an urgent need for radical reform in the total educational structure, fiscal reform should take into consideration the relationship between school spending and the provision of other government services for children and youth. Finally, in spite of the fact that many authorities think that the *Rodriguez* case and other trends will shift the action arena for removing inequities to state governments and away from federally supported programs, we must not lose sight of the gross inequities that exist from one state to another. It is in the national interest that states with lower financial resources for schools should receive assistance that will remove financial disparities. Why should any child who happens by chance to be born in a poor state have to receive less in the quality of his education?

Conclusion

We have come to a point in our national development where the educational institution, like most others, is in need of radical reform. The crisis in the cities has forced us to attempt various forms of school organization, four of which have been discussed in this chapter. In our plans for the future, we must clearly understand the educational goals we strive to achieve. We must provide quality education for children and youth. We must avoid becoming sidetracked by special interest groups and selfish political interests. We must strive for new forms of school organization which will enable teachers and administrators to develop more appropriate and effective learning environments.

Notes

1. Fred M. Hechinger, "Lawrence Cremin: Looking Toward the Heights," *Saturday Review World* (19 October 1974), p. 56.

2. David K. Cohen, "Policy for the Public Schools: Compensation and Integration," *Harvard Educational Review* 38 (1968): 137.

3. James S. Coleman et al., *Equality of Educational Opportunity* (Washington, D.C.: U.S. Government Printing Office, 1966).

4. U.S. Commission on Civil Rights, *Racial Isolation in the Public Schools* (Washington, D.C.: U.S. Government Printing Office, 1967), p. 67.

5. David Ausubel and Pearl Ausubel, "Ego Development among Segregated Negro Children," in *Education in Depressed Areas*, ed. A. Harry Passow (New York: Teachers College Press, Columbia University, 1963), p. 113.

6. "The largest number of compensatory program evaluations was brought together by the U.S. Commission on Civil Rights, *Racial Isolation in the Public Schools*, pp. 120-140. After reviewing the evaluations of various programs, none of which seemed to show any sustained academic improvement, the commission concluded that "the compensatory programs reviewed here appear to suffer from the defect inherent in attempting to solve problems stemming in part from racial and social class isolation in schools which themselves are isolated by race and social class." The report, however, noted proposals to double expenditures in city schools, and said that "short of such steps" compensation was unlikely to work.

7. Ibid.

8. Cohen, "Policy for the Public Schools," p. 139.

9. Allan C. Ornstein, Daniel U. Levine, and Doxey A. Wilkerson, *Reforming Metropolitan Schools* (Pacific Palisades, Calif.: Goodyear, 1975), p. 129.

10. Ibid.

11. Joint Center for Political Studies, unpublished material for the *National Roster of Black Elected Officials*, vol. 5, 1975, Washington, D.C.

12. Mel Ravitz, "Education Today and Tomorrow," in *Urban Education for the 1970s*, ed. A. Harry Passow (New York: Teachers College Press, Columbia University, 1971), p. 187.

13. John Dewey and Evelyn Dewey, *Schools of Tomorrow* (New York: Dutton, 1962), p. 225.

14. Serrano v. Priest, 5 Cal. 3d 584, 487 P.2d 1241 (1971).

15. Houston I. Flournoy, "Serrano and the Future of School Finance," *State Government* 44 (1972): 79-88.

16. Rodriguez v. San Antonio Independent School District, 337 F. Supp. 280 (W.D. Tex. 1971).

17. Joel S. Burke, *Answers to Inequity: An Analysis of the New School Finance* (Berkeley, Calif.: McCutchan, 1974), p. 15.

5 Who Controls the Schools?

James W. Guthrie and Patricia A. Craig

Answers to the question of who controls the schools are reminiscent of the descriptions of an elephant given by the five blind men. Their widely varying responses were shaped by each individual's experience with different features of the animal's anatomy. There also exist diverging views about the control of American schools, and perceptions of reality seem to be influenced greatly by an individual's position. Assume for a moment that a sample of parents, teachers, school board members, superintendents were asked the question "Who makes important decisions about schools in your community? The following hypothetical responses illustrate the point:

Parent: The answer is definitely the teachers. Last year our teaching staff went on strike for three weeks. They demanded higher salaries and control over curriculum development. In the end the strike was effective; the school board, over the objections of a large portion of the community, agreed to meet the teachers' demands. This forced tax increases and budget cuts in other areas to meet the salary commitment.

Teacher: The school board and the superintendent make the important decisions. The superintendent and his staff develop the district budget, and the school board must approve it. Only the school board can make decisions about salary increases and set district policy related to educational issues.

School board member: It is the state legislature. As school board members our powers are limited. We are bound by restrictive legislation and obligated to enforce all state mandates. It is the legislature that decides on matters such as what should be taught, what qualifications teachers must have before they can be hired, and the minimum number of days children must attend school. Most of our decisions simply reinforce or support the state education code drafted by the legislature.

Superintendent: It is voters who control the public schools. They vote for school board members and must approve tax increases and bond issues for building new schools. If they refuse to vote for tax increases, it is impossible for us to provide the best education for the children of this district. Because voters control the purse strings and the kind of people who are elected to the school board, they have powerful influence over what kind of decisions are made.

Such a foray into the realm of public opinion, while indeed interesting, is not likely to produce a clear answer to the question of school control. One of the problems with each of those answers is they do not reflect the complicated relationships between the various actors involved in school policy setting. One must extend the inquiry further to include such questions as: Who makes what kinds of decisions? and What is the impact of those decisions upon a school system? That is, what are the interactions between decisions and expenditure patterns, decisions and behaviors, decisions and school achievement, and so on.

A somewhat more systematic means for understanding the decision making process for schools is to trace the historical development of school control. Traditionally Americans have ascribed to the principle of subsidiarity in school governance, that is, to the belief that schools should leave most decisions to the smallest unit possible.[1] Thus, the hierarchy of school decision making can be thought of as an inverted pyramid (see Figure 5-1), with the greatest number of decisions being made by the family unit and progressively fewer decisions being made by teachers; principals; districts; and local, state, and federal governments. Historically this structure prevailed in the most literal sense in both the operation and maintenance of schools. During the middle and late 1800s, there were more than 100,000 school districts and approximately 1 school board member for every 138 people in the United States. This representative ratio provided an opportunity for community residents to have frequent and close contact with local school board members. Disagreements over school issues could be settled on a personal basis. Thus parents had substantial control over

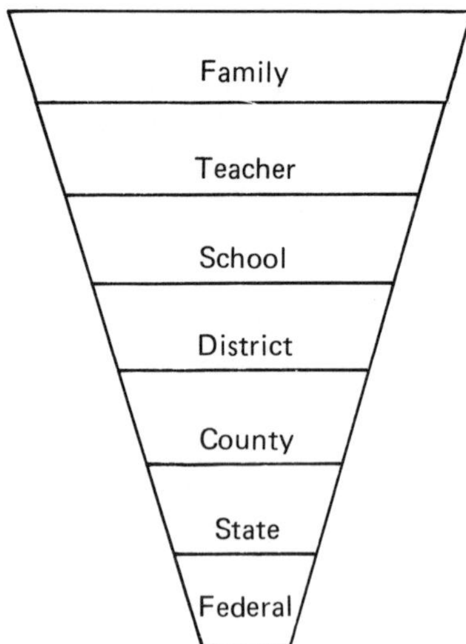

Figure 5-1. Theoretical Hierarchy of Decision Making in Schools

schooling. The transition into the twentieth century however brought significant changes. Corruption of governmental officials was uncovered at all levels by the turn-of-the-century "muckrakers."[2] Schools were not exempted from close examination and attack. Irregularities were exposed in the awarding of building contracts, the selection of textbooks, and the supplying of other materials. In addition, teaching positions often depended upon who, rather than what, one knew. The system of scandalous politics extended to the school level. Particularly in the cities, schools were frequently under the control of strongly partisan, ward-based political machines. In addition to these actual illegal practices, schools were also criticized for poor and inefficient management techniques.[3]

A call for school governance reform became part of the general crusade for "clean" government. In an attempt to insulate education from the evils of excessively partisan politics, school districts were designated as "special purpose governments," and connections with party politics were statutorily prevented in many states. School board members were forbidden to run as political party members, and school elections were moved to "off years" and "off months" in order to avoid contact with other elections. School boards were even granted their own taxing power in an attempt to free them from the slightest taint of political conflict. Paralleling such political reforms, an attempt was made to encourage more efficient school management. One result was a dramatic move to consolidate schools into large administrative units. The hope was to achieve vast economies of scale by merging districts. This shift proceeded rapidly, and by 1962 the number of school districts had been reduced from more than 100,000 to slightly more than 33,000. By 1974 the amount had shrunk to approximately 16,000, a reduction in the number of districts by more than half during a ten-year period.[4] These changes had a dramatic effect upon the governance of America's schools, particularly in terms of local control. Although school district consolidation perhaps reflects one of the greatest and most significant reform of local government, surprisingly it took place virtually unnoticed. As the reduction in the number of school districts proceeded, there was a consequent reduction in the number of school boards and thus in the number of school board trustees. At the same time the total population continued to increase. Therefore a wide disparity has evolved between representatives and their constituents. While each school board member once represented more than 100 people, by 1975 each school board member represented an average of 3,000 constituents. In large cities such as New York, Chicago, and Los Angeles, each school trustee represents literally millions of fellow residents. In addition, the attempts to depoliticize education were effective in establishing the view in the public's mind that school decisions should not be part of the political system. Thus, in many districts today school board elections are not highly visible as public offices and little is done to focus public attention on the school board selection process. In a recent survey of 500 board members and 82 school superintendents, L. Harmon Zeigler and N. Kent Jennings report that more than a third of the "elected" board members either were appointed to office or had no opposition on the ballot at the time of their election.[5]

The result of the changes has been an erosion of the ability of the family to influence decisions about schools and a substantial dilution of the personal contact between constituents and the policy making structure of schools. While it is true that such disparities have also occurred in other sectors of government, it can be argued that education is a public service more intimately tied to the daily lives of more citizens than any other. Public schools, in large measure, have been granted a monopoly. Thus, it is argued, the public needs to retain a substantial measure of control over them. And the continued movement toward political insulation of school decision makers and reduction of the client's ability to effect decisions should consequently be viewed with some alarm.

School district consolidation and efforts toward political reform abetted yet another movement which has had a serious impact upon school decision making. Those two reforms created an ideal atmosphere for the development of the "professional manager" and the "educational expert." The popular call for professionalization in school administration grew out of the corruption of the 1900s and paralleled a similar movement in municipal government, the evolution of the city manager plan. As school districts grew larger, budgets and the management process became substantially more complicated. No longer was it possible for the school board member to have intimate contact with either voters, parents, teachers, or children. Districts grew to incorporate many individual schools, and the complexity of their operation required boards to hire superintendents who could carry on the day-to-day operation of a large enterprise.[6]

Describing the situation prior to the 1900s, Joseph Cronin writes that "laymen ran the schools the way they wanted to run them, delegating to school men only the more esoteric problems of curriculum and supervision. Most personnel, maintenance, and business matters were handled by lay boards without professional consultation."[7] The school superintendent was expected, in theory, only to implement policy determined and mandated by the school boards. The superintendent was thought to be a caretaker rather than an educator. He was expected to supervise the building of schools, allocate supplies, and keep accurate records. In practice, however, the superintendency has pyramided into an extremely powerful position possessing substantial influence over school board policy. This is due, in part, to the superintendent's control over the flow of information and the preparation and presentation of budgetary materials to the school board. Not only does the superintendent have the ability to present or withhold information, but also he is expected to suggest policy alternatives. Thus Frederick Wirt and Michael Kirst write: "The superintendent often defines issues, proposes alternatives, provides technical ammunition for his supporters, and in the end implements or evades the decisions arrived at [by the board]."[8] As school systems have responded to these changes, the effect has been to permit many day-to-day decisions to be dominated by the professional manager. The ability of the family to make decisions has become limited to voting for school board members and on tax and bond issues. Some may argue (as the superintendent did in the hypothetical response at the beginning of this chapter) that the public's ability to vote on these matters has a crucial impact upon the governance of schools. However, such a view requires making normative judgments about the nature of decisions. For example, is it more important to a family to be able to vote for or against bonds or taxes than it is for them to choose the school or the teacher their child will have?

As school systems have evolved and come under the dominance of professional managers and educational experts, teachers too have been affected. They have lost their ability to communicate easily with their employers. The opportunity for a teacher to talk directly with a school trustee or even with the superintendent and his staff is increasingly rare. This triggered feelings of alienation and inefficacy on the part of teachers. While responsible for the actual delivery of educational services to children, they frequently believed they had little control over what was taught or what texts and techniques would be used. Thus, teachers also found themselves unable to participate in decisions that affected them directly. However, teachers, unlike school boards, parents, or voters, have succeeded somewhat better in seeking a solution to their problem. By joining together collectively in various organizations, teachers have begun to exercise substantial influence and veto power over school decision making. Part of their new found control rests in collective bargaining and in a threat to withhold their services. Because of the effectiveness of teachers in obtaining power, it is no longer possible for a school board in a large city, such as New York, Chicago, or Los Angeles, to enact or implement a new policy without the teacher's spokesman consent. If, for example, a strike or the threat of a strike does not sway a board's decision, teachers can always resort to direct political action. Teachers have shown themselves to be quite potent in this latter regard. Both at the federal level and in a number of states, teacher organizations report the largest dollar contribution to political campaigns of any registered lobbies. And as a last resort, teachers can refuse to implement policy in the classroom.

These changes in the power of teachers have come partially at the expense of their image as dedicated professionals. In no state are teachers actually granted legal authority to strike. Thus, by participating in strikes, teachers have often broken the law. Strike activities have continued to proliferate. Between 1955 and 1966 there were only 35 strikes. During the year 1967-68 there were 114 strikes affecting twenty-one states and involving over 163,000 teachers. This strike activity resulted in the loss of 1.4 million teacher working days. In the folowing year the number of strikes increased to 131, almost doubling the loss in teaching time.[9]

Beside the question of who controls the schools, there is the question of who has the *authority* to control the schools. Though important, the question is no easier to answer than the first. School governments, because they are considered *special purpose districts* are in a distinctly ambiguous position. The nature of the special district is to restrict the power of the legislative body. While all local governmental units are, theoretically, agents of state government, city councils and county governments have substantial flexibility in the control they are permitted to exercise over local matters. Cities are free to determine their own property tax rates and can initiate a wide range of additional taxes if required to meet fiscal needs. However, the school districts have restricted taxing power and for the most part are limited to taxing only real property. Another constraint is that large proportions of the school budget are often restricted by state statute and may only be used for specific categorical purposes. For example, California's state education code requires that at least 55 percent of a school district's budget must be spent for teachers' salaries. Municipal governments seldom are subject to such restrictions. Thus, while schools in a legal sense are special purpose districts with the single goal in mind of educating children, functionally they provide comprehensive general services. Schools are responsible for the immediate health and safety of children and provide recreation, food services, counseling, vocational training, and so on. However, legal limitations on the authority that may be exercised at the local level undermine the ability of the public to shape the nature of these school services.

The question of who has the authority to control schools is not one that legislators like to discuss; it requires addressing questions about who should make which decisions. It is also an area that has been avoided by most academic scholars. In the past this latter group has been content to examine the easier question of who does make decisions. However, what appears to be more necessary is a rethinking of the school governance system based upon a classification of each actor's interest or claims upon the system. Which issues fall within the interest of the federal, state, and local governments? Can issues be specified over which the family should have controlling interest? Which issues are the legitimate claim of teachers and administrators? It will be difficult to draw clear distinctions because there are overlapping areas of concern to all, although one concern presumably shared by all constituents is the child. The simplified schematic in Table 5-1 outlines common interests as well as individual concerns.

The governance structure of America's public schools needs serious reappraisal. There is little consensus by either the public or researchers regarding who does control the schools and almost no serious consideration of who *should* control the schools. Since the yearly 1900s patterns of governance, born of reform, have tended to provide opportunities to some groups to participate and share decisions while creating obstacles for others, namely, laymen and the general public. As yet there has not been a systematic study of governance patterns in American public schools which explores the political, social, and educational effects upon the system. However, several independently developed

Table 5-1
Interests and Functions of All Parties Concerned with the School System

Party	Interests and Functions
Federal government	Protection of individual rights Assurance of equality of opportunity Establishing national goals Regime maintenance
State government	Establishment of educational institutions Establishing and enforcing minimum educational standards Regime maintenance
School district	Reflection of local values Carrying out state mandates Serve as locus of political interaction
Parents	Concern for future of children Development of social, intellectual, and vocational competence
Teachers	Maintenance of professional standards Improvement of working conditions Concern for the student (overlap of all interests)
Children	Social interchange

strategies have been suggested that have important implications for school governance. One of these is the development of a professional hierarchy for teachers, such as that suggested by the Fleischmann Commission in New York State.[10] At present teaching is remarkably unspecialized and there is little recognition of different levels of expertise within teaching which can be rewarded with differential salary based upon competency. Another reform that, according to proponents, could have the effect of establishing lines of authority and assuring accountability in schools is the so-called performance contract. This is an agreement between a school district and contracting organization calling for reimbursement or a bonus to the contractor on the basis of measured performance of students. Under some circumstances teachers and groups of teachers have acted as the contractor.[11] The voucher system, another alternative, has the potential for introducing greater family choice into the governance system. Vouchers are essentially educational warrants issued to parents who are thereafter free to choose whichever school they want their children to attend. Since the success or failure of schools depends upon the parents' evaluation of school performance, added productivity as well as choice are alleged as important benefits of such a scheme.[12] Finally, a promising alternative for modifying the structure of decision making within schools, which would also clarify roles of responsibility and accountability, is school-site budgeting. Such a plan calls for lump sums to be allocated by the district to the local school, with few local strings attached, for the development and management of its own educational program. School-site budgeting requires community cooperation from teachers, parents, and the school principal in the establishment of goals and the determination of spending priorities. This reform assumes the utility of the principle of subsidiarity, that is, decisions that impinge directly upon the local school are best made at the local school site.[13] The voucher system is similarly rooted in the ideology of subsidiarity but uses the family, rather than the school site, as the locus of decision making.

Conclusion

The common factor in all these suggested reforms is that they seek a realignment of decision making power. They provide increased professional autonomy on matters of instruction for the teacher and substantial choice for the client. Also, they posit models for compromise between laymen and professionals at the local school site rather than at a more remote and isolated district office. Unfortunately, little research has been done to measure the impact of governance options upon possible policy outcomes. Should school districts be given the same flexibility as city and county governments to direct the delivery of educational services? What are the implications of such reforms? Can the ambiguous role of the school board be changed within the current context of educational governance to more clearly establish lines of authority and accountability? Because a discussion of reform possibilities triggers even more questions about who controls American schools, the present-day confusion about school governance is underscored. And we are, essentially, back to the question with which this chapter opened.

Notes

1. John E. Coons, William E. Clune III, and Stephen D. Sugarman, *Private Wealth and Public Education* (Cambridge, Mass.: Harvard University Press, 1970).

2. Joseph M. Cronin, *The Control of Urban Schools* (New York: Free Press, 1973).

3. For evidence of this, see David Tyack, *The One Best System: A History of American Urban Education* (Cambridge, Mass.: Harvard University Press, 1974).

4. National Center for Educational Statistics, *A Century of Public School Statistics* (Washington, D.C.: U.S. Government Printing Office, 1974).

5. L. Harmon Zeigler and N. Kent Jennings, *Governing American Schools* (North Scituate, Mass.: Duxbury Press, 1975).

6. Raymond Callahan, *Education and The Cult of Efficiency* (Chicago: University of Chicago Press, 1962).

7. Cronin, *The Control of Urban Schools*, pp. 9-10.

8. Frederick M. Wirt and Michael Kirst, *The Political Web of American Schools* (Boston: Little, Brown & Co., 1972), p. 92.

9. See NEA Research Division, *Negotiation Research Digest, 1966-69* (Washington, D.C.: National Education Association, 1966-69).

10. *The Fleischmann Report on the Quality, Cost and Financing of Elementary and Secondary Education in New York State*, vol. 3 (New York: Viking Press, 1973).

11. For a description of performance contracting, see Leon Lessinger, "Every Kid A Winner: Accountability in Education," *Contemporary Psychology* 18 (1973): 344-345.

12. For a discussion of voucher plan possibilities, see Christopher Jencks, "Giving Parents Money for Schooling: Education Vouchers," *Phi Delta Kappan* 52 (1970): 49-52, and idem, "Is The Public School Obsolete," *The Public Interest* 2 (1966): 18-27.

13. A description of school site budgeting and a review of related research findings is provided by Norman J. Seward in "Centralized and Decentralized School Budgeting: A Comparative Analysis" (Ph.D. diss., University of California, Berkeley).

Student Achievement, Teacher Behavior, and Accountability

Harry L. Miller

Accountability–that is, making schools responsible for the achievement of specified objectives–appears to be the major educational battle of the 1970s, supplanting the arguments of the 1960s over the liberation of the classroom. The romantic attack on the schools in the earlier period was merely a more extreme and ferocious expression of a humanistic tradition that began in the nineteenth century. Important elements in the current demands for accountability seem startlingly new, and one must dig hard in the history of the American school to find a few scattered attempts to base teacher salaries on results. Although the humanist and egalitarian thrusts during the 1960s often appeared around similar issues, it is now clear that they rest on substantially different assumptions and share only a rather simplistic view of the relation of the individual to complex social institutions.

History, even recent history, provides a useful perspective. There is little question that, if ten years of compensatory education had shown any signal success in reducing the achievement gap between lower-class minority children and the national achievement norms, we would not now be seeing state legislatures, notoriously slow to act on most major issues, passing school accountability laws with the speed at which they normally approve appropriations for their own expense accounts. Compensatory education did fail. A judgment of how badly it failed depends on the temperament of the observer, how much evaluation research he reads, and how carefully he reads it. But the general professional judgment is fairly solid. Significantly, most of the extra resources applied to the schools in the course of compensatory treatments consist of human resources in the form of additional instruction by trained teachers or paraprofessionals. The profession itself obviously was convinced that more and better teaching would close the performance gap that compensatory education was attempting to deal with.

The disillusionment with compensatory education among educators and the informed public has taken three major forms:

1. A chastened optimism, particularly among those who have a considerable stake in the elaborate network of federal and state financed projects operating under the compensatory umbrella. Those who chose this response[1] have lowered their expectation levels but taken heart from the evidence available that, at least on the macrocosmic level, marginal gains can be reaped from compensatory efforts.

2. An acceptance of social reality on the part of those who view a decade of compensatory efforts as a genuine disaster and are unwilling to accept the high cost of the marginal gains that may be obtained by their continuance. The general view of those taking this approach is that social and economic gains of minority groups will eventually, over a generation perhaps, make the schooling issue moot.[2]

3. A search for alternatives based on a sense of frustration and a conviction that far from being *incapable* of closing the performance gap between minority and mainstream children, the public schools are *unwilling* to do what is necessary to achieve that goal. The causes are variously attributed to the stifling and stingy bureaucracy of the urban systems; the racism of teachers, or their lack of skill, or their laziness; the job-protectiveness of staff unions; the ineptitude of teacher training institutions; the unfairness of civil service systems, and the cruelly misleading theories of social scientists.[3]

Whatever the imputed cause, this disillusionment has grown rapidly into a fairly cohesive doctrine of educational accountability. In the voucher system proposals, the doctrine holds the school accountable to the individual parent. In performance contracting schemes, it holds an outside agent accountable to the school system. In community control, it holds the schools accountable to parents as a group. And in competency-based programs, it holds the individual teacher and the school accountable to the state department of education.

The Battleground

According to a survey by the Educational Testing Service, all but four states now have on their books or are planning an educational accountability program. As of 1974, thirty-two states already had passed such laws.[4] When an accounting of the various laws is made, it is likely that about half of them will require some assessment of student progress as a measure of teacher performance. In an instance that carries the movement's idea to its ultimate absurdity, the case of a California adolescent who is suing a school system because he graduated from high school unable to read above an elementary school level is working its way through the courts.

On an allied front, the majority of state departments of education have mandated a system of performance or competency-based teacher education that shares the basic assumption of accountability laws, that pupil achievement level is, or can be, fundamentally determined by the measurable behavior of teachers. Once made, that assumption logically resolves into an insistence that teacher training institutions produce teacher behavior that, in the classroom, will achieve the equality of results sought by the accountability statutes.[5]

Is it absurd to demand equal results from equal teacher input? To what extent can we expect "teaching to count"? One of the many difficulties with the recent debate over the question of whether teaching counts is the muddled way the question is often framed. No one in his right mind would suggest that any child exposed to systematic, continuous instruction will not learn more than another child deprived of that instruction. Nor would anyone dispute the likelihood that average achievement levels of children instructed for ten months a year will exceed those of children exposed to such instruction for seven months. Nor the likelihood that a national school system that insists on six years of instruction in mathematics will produce children with higher levels of mathematical skill than a system that requires three years of math. The literature of the debate is dotted with such efforts to prove that teaching makes a difference by showing that the length of the school year or number of required courses correlate with achievement.[6]

In the context of the accountability movement these are not the issues. The question that must be addressed is: How much of the variation in student achievement can be accounted for by differences in teacher behavior when other sources for the variation in achievement are held constant? Or, more specifically, given the same quantity of instruction, with pupils of the same social class level and subject to the same parental pressure to achieve, can we predict that an identified set of teacher behaviors will get appreciably better results than another?

Attempts to settle the question with large-scale correlational studies, such as Coleman's survey of equal educational opportunity[7] or Jencks' study of the equalizing impact of schooling,[8] have largely failed to persuade. Evidence that school systems have little differential impact may obscure real differences in effectiveness among individual teachers within each system. If the focus is narrowed to schools as the unit of analysis, as in the evaluation studies of the More Effective School Program in New York, classroom observation is likely to find, as those studies did, that most teachers do not adopt "innovative" behaviors.[9]

There remains one large body of research that has a direct bearing on the issue, the results of an attempt to define "good" teaching or "good" teaching style by concentrating on teacher characteristics, with the individual teacher as the unit of study. Fifty years of effort has by now been devoted to that research, and it speaks directly to the point at issue.

Teaching Behavior and Student Achievement

In their 1971 review of the research on teacher performance, Barak Rosenshine and Norma Furst begin by saying that "this review is an admission that we know very little about the relationship between classroom behavior and student gains." But they go on to argue that can the research findings at least point to the directions that future work might find most fruitful. The field is a confused one, they admit; so much so, that it is not unusual to find different institutions training teachers to opposite criteria.[10]

Rosenshine and Furst note at length the difficulties in assessing the results of a variety of research types. Laboratory studies of teaching cannot very easily be generalizable to actual classes of children. Research on the teaching of subject matters tends to compare only a few teachers and to use the individual student as the sampling unit, which makes them largely useless for the purpose of teacher behavior comparisons. Experimental classroom studies in which instructional procedures are varied and student performance assessed seldom are well enough controlled to permit useful generalization. The review concentrates, then, on a fourth type of study, *process-product research*, which relates observable teacher behaviors to student achievement measures. There are, to be sure, some measurement problems. Some of the studies use *low-inference* observations of teachers, very specific behavioral descriptions ("teacher repeats student's idea"). And others use *high-inference* observations requiring the observer to make a general rating on the basis of a number of events ("clarity of presentation–high"). Low-inference observations are more reliable and easier to handle because they result in a quantitative measure of the number of times a teacher produces the given behavior. But such observations are sometimes difficult to connect to some more general variable of teacher behavior. Furthermore, the most consistent relationships found between teacher behavior and student achievement are those based on high-inference observations, which are the least reliable.

The authors note another major problem of the research format: the difficulty of making causal inferences from correlational data. Some of the cited studies, for example, find a relation between the number of negative comments from teachers and the achievement of their pupils–the more negative the teachers, the less achievement on the part of the pupils. This finding makes a good fit with current fashions in teaching style, but it may reflect only the likelihood that teachers with low-achieving classes have little to approve and much to criticize.

From forty-two available process-product studies Rosenshine and Furst select eleven teacher variables that they consider "most promising," that is, teacher behaviors that appear to relate to achievement with correlations that exceed chance. (It is of interest to note the variables that do *not* appear promising, because many are considered crucial by some advocates of accountability: nonverbal approval, praise, warmth, the ratio of all indirect behaviors to all direct teacher behaviors, flexibility, the amount of teacher talk versus student talk, student participation, number of student-teacher interactions, student absence, teacher absence, teacher time spent on class participation, teacher experience, and teacher knowledge of the subject area.)

Of the following eleven variables that do appear promising, Rosenshine and

Furst specify the first five as having "strong support" from the correlational studies. The last six, while having less support, appear to deserve further study.

1. clarity
2. variability (variety of methods, approaches, and so on)
3. enthusiasm
4. task-oriented or businesslike behaviors or both
5. student opportunity to learn what is later tested
6. use of student ideas and general indirectness
7. criticism (negative relation)
8. use of structuring comments (summarizing, the use of verbal markers, and so on)
9. types of questions (though exactly what type is best is at the moment unclear)
10. probing
11. level of difficulty of instruction

The rather small, but apparently solid, cause for optimism thus opened up by Rosenshine and Furst has since been systematically extinguished by Robert Heath and Mark Nielson in a more detailed and rigorous examination of the same group of studies.[11] Their paper goes well beyond the surface findings to assess the adequacy of the research in order to judge the degree of confidence that can reasonably be assigned to those findings. They checked each of the eleven variables selected as promising by Rosenshine and Furst for the validity of the relation between the operational definition used to measure the teacher behavior and the variable itself. Heath and Nielson found such disparities as a classroom rating of *difficulty of the lesson* cited as a measure of *clarity*. In their judgment, nearly a third of the operational definitions did not correspond to the variables that later included them.

They also rated the research design that formed the basis for a total of seventy-eight citations of the eleven variables. Only five of the seventy-eight citations were derived from studies that used random assignment of pupils to treatments, yet the studies employed a statistical analysis whose interpretation implies the use of randomization. Even so, a majority (forty-five out of seventy-eight) of the citations did not claim to find a significant relation between the variable cited and student achievement. For many of the variables, negative or clearly nonsignificant relationships were reported.

For each of the relationships cited in all forty-two studies, Heath and Nielson provide data on a number of analytic cautionary measures that should have been taken. They conclude: "Critically important assumptions such as linearity, normality, homogeneity of variance, and parallel slopes are almost universally unreported. There is reason to believe that in many instances these assumptions are *not*, in fact, tenable."[12]

Finally, they note that two important types of variables which might well have influenced the relationships cited were not controlled:

Though the studies reviewed . . . were concerned with everything from aircraft mechanics to reading, no effort is apparent in identifying the possible interactions between teacher-behavior variables and content. It seems unlikely that *one* set of teaching behaviors is most effective for teaching everything. If there is an important interaction between type of content and teaching behavior (given cognitive achievement as criteria), then the conclusion about which teaching behavior is effective may be determined as much by content as by teacher behavior. . . . Despite persistent evidence that variables such as socioeconomic status and ethnic status are more important determinants of average achievement level than teacher behavior, the research on teacher-behavior variables largely ignores such differences among students. Similarly, the studies cited by Rosenshine and Furst cover a wide student age range (preschool to adult), yet the idea that effective teacher behavior might be different for different age groups is ignored when conclusions are drawn from such collections. It seems unlikely that one set of teacher behaviors is most effective for teaching everything to everybody.[13]

Heath and Nielson also provide a valuable service in collating the conclusions of a number of earlier reviews of the research on teacher characteristics and student achievement—Brim: "no consistent relation between any characteristics, including intelligence, and teaching effectiveness"[14]; Dubin and Taveggia: "demonstrate clearly and unequivocally that there is no measurable difference among truly distinctive methods of college instruction"[15]; Mood: "at the present moment we cannot make any sort of meaningful quantitative estimate of the effect of teachers on student achievement"[16]; Getzels and Jackson: "very little is known for certain about the nature and measurement of teacher personality, or about the relation between teacher personality and teaching effectiveness"[17]; Wallen and Travers: "the best one might hope for would be slight differences in teaching effectiveness within narrow aspects of the learning process, and this is roughly what is found by empirical research."[18]

Commenting on the findings of his own review, Jim Stephens makes the following acute observation on the meaningfulness of the evidence:

. . . insensitive as the tests may be and over-controlled or under-controlled as some experiments probably are and exacting as standards undoubtedly are, a great deal of growth does appear and does meet the standards. The investigations cited do not fail to reveal growth. They merely fail to reveal differences in growth attributable to the administrative (teaching) variables. If we use other variables, such as background factors, moreover, marked differences in growth also come through. If the tests, and the designs, and the criteria of significance permit such differences to appear, it is difficult to see why they should not also permit differences in administrative (teaching) factors to come through if these were present.[19]

Teacher Expectancy Effects

The accountability advocate is likely to respond to such a clear demonstration of the absence of an empirical base for differential teacher impact by arguing that the impact is influenced by much more subtle mechanisms than are usually measured in such studies. The most popular current explanation for differences in achievement between white middle-class students and lower-class minorities indicts the teacher for having lower expectations of achievement for the latter groups, an hypothesis often referred to as the "self-fulfilling prophecy," or the "Pygmalion effect." The idea that such teachers not only slacken their own teaching efforts but also communicate a sense of inevitable failure to their minority pupils was widely disseminated by Kenneth Clark and led to the Rosenthal and Jacobson study, now so well known that it need not be described here.[20] In the five or six years since that study's publication, approximately sixty studies relating to the expectancy effect have been done, making it one of the most popular topics in the educational research literature.

The most comprehensive and detailed argument for the importance of teacher expectancy effects may be found in Jere Brophy and Thomas Goode's *Teacher-Student Relationships.*[21] The following assessment of the evidence they offer is focused on one particular body of studies, those that use school achievement, or some student behavior reasonably related to school achievement, as the criterion measure. This restriction is a crucial one. There is massive evidence that school learning is systematically influenced by family environment, social class differences, and individual ability, which are not likely to be important determinants of marble-dropping, sociometric status, the types of story that children tell, or other criteria commonly employed in studying the expectancy effect.

Brophy and Goode provide a model for these effects that runs as follows: first, teachers form early in the school year differential expectations regarding the achievement potential of their pupils; on the basis of these expectations, they treat students differently; pupils reciprocally respond to this teacher treatment in ways that reinforce the teacher's expectation and, over time, will gradually approximate the expectations more and more closely.

The hypothesis requires either the demonstration of a direct relationship between teacher expectations and student achievement or, more satisfactorily, a showing of several linkages—between teacher expectation and teacher behavior *and* between teacher behavior and student expectation of his or her own achievement. The following section explores the evidence for a direct relation between expectation and achievement whether or not there is any demonstration of the processes that connect the two variables.

Induced Teacher Expectations

The largest number of studies of the expectancy effect follow the Rosenthal and Jacobson model: teachers are given, in some plausible form, information that they are to expect a higher level of achievement from a certain group of children who have in fact been selected at random. Table 6-1 lists all such studies using an academic criterion measure considered by Brophy and Goode. Their eagerness to prove the expectancy effect ensures that any research available that attained significant results is included.[22] The entry N.S. indicates findings that failed to support the existence of the relationship between teacher expectation and student achievement; significant positive results, without regard to magnitude, are indicated by Sig. Dashes signify that data on the process link between teacher expectation and teacher behavior is not provided.

Of eleven classroom studies, only one, using air force cadets in mathematic sections, attained significance, a proportion of positive to negative findings that one could almost expect by chance. Two experimental studies using ten-minute

Table 6-1
Studies of Experimentally Induced Teacher Expectations with Academic Achievement Criteria

Study	Situation	Relation between Teacher Expectation and Student Achievement	Relation between Teacher Expectation and Teacher Behavior
Anderson and Rosenthal	Summer camp	n.s.	neg.
Beez	Experimental (10 min.)	sig.	sig.
Brown	Tutoring	n.s.	sig.
Carter	Experimental (10 min.)	sig.	sig.
Claiborn	Classroom	n.s.	—
Conn, Edwards, Rosenthal, and Crowne	Classroom	n.s.	—
Evans and Rosenthal	Classroom	n.s.	—
Fielder, Cohen, and Feeney	Classroom	n.s.	—
Fleming and Anttonen	Classrom	n.s.	—
Flowers	Classroom	mixed	—
Goldsmith and Fry	Classroom	n.s.	—
Jose and Cody	Classroom	n.s.	n.s.
Kester and Letchworth	Classroom	n.s.	sig.
Meichenbaum, Bowers, and Ross	Tutoring	sig.	sig.
Panda and Guskin	Experimental (10 min.)	n.s.	n.s.
Pellegrini and Hicks	Tutoring	n.s.	—
Pitt	Classroom	n.s.	—
Schrank	Classroom	sig.	—

periods of the simplest possible form of word learning had significant results, as did one of the tutoring studies. These are the only positive studies for which both product and process findings were significant. And in the case of Meichenbaum, Bowers, and Ross, the study was based on four teachers and fourteen students. Note also that in two of the five cases in which teachers behaved as if responding to the induced expectation, the behavior had no measurable effect on student achievement.

Brophy and Goode attribute these negative results to a number of factors, including the difficulty of getting teachers to accept false data in the face of their own experience with students, and the possibility that some of them may have been aware of the experimental design. The authors suggest that where the expectancies were not introduced until midyear, one semester might not be enough time for them to become effective, although they seem willing to accept positive results in other studies where the expectancy operated for only ten minutes. In any event, their conclusion that it is time to relinquish the Pygmalion induced-expectation design seems accurate.

Natural Teacher Expectations

On the other hand, that design was developed to circumvent one enormous difficulty in trying to measure the effect of teacher expectancy in natural settings, namely, that teacher expectations are, most of the time, realistic assessments of a child's ability to achieve. Most of the evidence reviewed by Brophy and Goode in this area is so contaminated by this real-life relationship that it is hardly worth discussing.

As an example, a British study by John Douglas[23] is nominated by Brophy and Goode as the "most definitive and compelling." Douglas reports a three-year follow-up study of children who had been assigned to academic tracks at the age of eight. Some of the children had been "misplaced" into either upper or lower tracks, if "correct" placement is defined by their measured performance. Three years later Douglas found that those who had been misplaced into higher sections improved, while those misplaced into lower sections deteriorated. This interesting finding is interpreted by Brophy and Goode as strong support for their thesis; it may be equally or more plausibly interpreted as a tribute to the prediction ability of teachers thoroughly familiar with individual children and consequently able to take a wider range of variables into account.

Support for the latter assumption may be found in an attempt by Bruce Tuckman and Martin Bierman to produce the same situation by manipulation.[24] In assigning students to tracks in junior and senior high school, the experimenters assigned control students on the basis of measured ability but allocated some low-ability students to medium tracks and some medium-ability students to high tracks. Achievement test scores of the experimental students did not significantly differ from their control counterparts. Brophy and Goode, oddly, make this sound like a triumphant vindication of their expectancy thesis because the *trends* in scores favored the experimentals, a striking example of the triumph of experimenter bias over error variance.

A short study by Palardy[25] is much more convincing and is the only evidence dealing with the natural expectations of teachers that is very persuasive. Palardy found five teachers who believed that there was no sex difference in reading ability and five who believed that boys could not learn to read as well as girls. The author matched the teachers in pairs to control for sex, experience, race, type of school, and reading text used. He found that the reading scores for boys were lower in the classes of those teachers who expected a sex difference than in the classes of teachers who did not expect such a difference. Unfortunately, the study has not been replicated.

Teacher Expectation-Teacher Behavior

A crucial link in Brophy and Goode's hypothesis is the establishment of a relationship between teacher expectation and differential teacher behavior; if such a relation does not operate systematically, the model falls apart. The general design of the best of the studies examining this relationship involves asking teachers for a listing of students from whom they expect high-level achievement and those from whom they expect lower level achievement. Observations of teacher behavior directed toward each type of student is then collected. Five studies of this kind reviewed by Brophy and Goode yield somewhat inconsistent results:

1. For the hypothesis that teachers pay *more attention* to high expectancy students, three studies yielded positive findings and one study, negative findings.
2. For the hypothesis that teachers *interact more* with high expectancy students—two positive, two negative.
3. For the hypothesis that teachers *praise* high expectancy students more—three positive, one negative.
4. For the hypothesis that teachers direct more criticism to low expectancy students—three negative, one positive.[26]

Brophy and Goode themselves conducted a series of studies using the same basic design, the results of which strikingly demonstrate the ambiguity of the hypothesis, the danger of relying on small-sample research, the crucial role of replication, and the resistance of dogged faith in a hypothesis to even one's own empirical evidence. Their first study sampled four ability-grouped classrooms at the first grade level ($N = 4$ teachers).[27] The teachers were asked to rank their students in order of expected achievement, and six of their high rankings and six of their low rankings were selected for observation. In support of the theory, high-expectancy children were praised more often for correct answers, criticized less often for incorrect answers, and given more cues by the teacher to help find the right answer or the solution to a problem. Low-expectancy children were given only the advantage of getting more feedback statements.

Brophy and Goode replicated the study, again with first grade classes, but with nine classrooms, nonability grouped. They report: "few of the findings from the initial study were replicated in the follow-up. As a group, teachers in the follow-up study showed no evidence of favoring highs or of treating them more appropriately than lows. If anything, the opposite was true." Indeed, the most solid finding of the second study demonstrated that, although highs sought more responses from teachers, teachers attempted "to compensate by calling on lows more frequently and especially by frequently initiating work-related contacts with them."[28]

It would be difficult to conclude from all these attempts that there is any more empirical ground for asserting a teacher expectancy effect on achievement on the basis of five years of study than there is for a more general differential impact of teaching style on the basis of fifty years of study.

The Future of Policy

The education accountability policy, if applied to medicine, would demand equal curative powers for a given treatment applied by a doctor. Without evidence that a treatment-result equality is any more likely to occur in education than in medicine, what can be expected as a consequence? The answer seems to be that political pressures will mediate between reality and the absurdity of the policy. When the state of Michigan decreed that state allocation of funds be made to school districts on condition that each district demonstrate improvement in student achievement levels, Detroit schools failed the test.[29] Were state appropriations to Detroit lowered as a result? In the words of Liza Doolittle, "Not bloody likely!" That Michigan's state superintendent of education went on to attest to a Congressional committee the glowing success of his accountability plan is a testimony to the political magic that makes policy failure into policy success simply by asserting it publicly.

What is most likely to happen is the adoption of an accountability process that operates within the well-established boundaries of predictable achievement levels for different groups of students. Such a model has been adopted by New York City as a result, to a considerable degree, of the pressure exerted by a strong and sophisticated union.[30] The model includes not only school processes and student achievement outputs but also inputs in the form of student characteristics and the environmental conditions of the home and community.

The determination of any policy requires a consideration of not only the preferences of the policy maker (everyone can agree that it would be desirable for all children to learn at an acceptable level) but also the probability that the preferred outcome can be achieved. The accountability movement demonstrates clearly the degree to which educational policy continues to be made on the basis of myth instead of estimated real probabilities. If industrial or military policy were similarly decided on the basis of preference without regard to what is possible, our viability as a nation would drop to zero. It is possible that, whatever the outcome of the accountability battle, the profession will have at least one positive gain to show for it—it may discard its fantasies of omnipotence in favor of a more mature and realistic sense of its limitations.

Conclusion

That is surely the lesson that educators should have learned from the turmoil of the sixties, filled with dizzying expectations about the power of institutions to shape people to anyone's desire, every extravagant hope of the reformers followed by equally extravagant experiments ending in verdicts of "no significant difference," "only marginal gains," "inconclusive results." Perhaps it is politically unfeasible in a period radically marked by high social expectations to relinquish the fantasy of omnipotence; perhaps educational reformers are temperamentally incapable of relinquishing it.

The current reform movement that has adopted accountability as a slogan appears to be more realistic than that of the past decade because it uses the "hard" language of program planning and management by objectives. But it has not yet learned, as the world of industrial and government management from which the models were borrowed *has* learned, that policy objectives can seldom be optimal and that we must settle most of the time for ones that are merely satisfactory. We may learn in the next decade of experimentation with educational accountability that we will either have to put up with results that are not even satisfactory, or reduce our expectations to conform with what we can, in a real sense, accomplish.

Notes

1. See, for example, the statement by Elliott Richardson as quoted in James Welsh, "Compensatory Education: Still More Funds," *Educational Researcher* 1 (1972): 13-14.

2. Robert Havighurst, "Curriculum for the Disadvantaged," *Phi Delta Kappan* 52 (1970): 371-373.

3. The most influential statement of these themes may be found in the speeches, articles, and books of Kenneth B. Clark; see, for example, *Dark Ghetto* (New York: Harper & Row, 1965).

4. Phyllis Hawthorne, *Legislation By the States: Accountability and Assess-*

ment in Education (Madison, Wis.: Wisconsin State Department of Public Instruction, 1973).

5. Allen A. Schmieder, *Competency-Based Education: The State of the Scene* (Washington, D.C.: American Association of Colleges for Teacher Education, 1973).

6. For an example, see Herbert J. Walberg and Sue P. Rasher, "Public School Effectiveness and Equality: New Evidence and Its Implications," *Phi Delta Kappan* 56 (1974): 3-9; and Davaed E. Wiley and Annegart A. Harmschfeger, "Explosion of a Myth," *Educational Researcher* 3 (1974): 7-12.

7. James S. Coleman et al., *Equality of Educational Opportunity* (Washington, D.C.: U.S. Government Printing Office, 1966).

8. Christopher Jencks et al., *Inequality: A Reassessment of the Effect of Family and Schooling in America* (New York: Basic Books, 1972).

9. David J. Fox, *Expansion of the More Effective School Program* (New York: Center for Urban Education, 1967).

10. Barak Rosenshine and Norma Furst, "Research in Teacher Performance Criteria," in *Research in Teacher Education*, ed. B.O. Smith (Englewood Cliffs, N.J.: Prentice-Hall, 1971), pp. 37-72.

11. Robert W. Heath and Mark A. Nielson, "The Research Basis for Performance-Based Teacher Education," *Review of Educational Research* 44 (1974): 463-484. Copyright 1974, American Educational Research Association, Washington, D.C.

12. Ibid., p. 476.

13. Ibid., pp. 476-477.

14. Orville G. Brim, *Sociology and the Field of Education* (New York: Russell Sage Foundation, 1958).

15. Robert Dubin and Thomas C. Taveggia, *The Teacher-Learning Paradox: A Comparative Analysis of College Teaching Methods* (Eugene, Or.: Center for the Advanced Study of Educational Administration, University of Oregon, 1968).

16. Alexander Mood, "Do Teachers Make a Difference?" in *Do Teachers Make a Difference? A Report on Recent Research in Pupil Achievement* (Washington, D.C.: U.S. Government Printing Office, 1970).

17. Jacob W. Getzels and Philip W. Jackson, "The Teacher's Personality and Characteristics," in *Handbook of Research on Teaching*, ed. N.L. Gage (Chicago: Rand McNally, 1963), pp. 506-582.

18. Norman E. Wallen and Robert M.W. Travers, "Analysis and Investigation of Teaching Methods," in *Handbook of Research on Teaching*, ed. N.L. Gage (Chicago: Rand McNally, 1963), pp. 448-505.

19. John M. Stephens, *The Process of Schooling* (New York: Holt, Rinehart and Winston, 1967), pp. 83-84.

20. Robert Rosenthal and Lenore Jacobson, *Pygmalion in the Classroom* (New York: Holt, Rinehart and Winston, 1968).

21. Jere E. Brophy and Thomas L. Goode, *Teacher-Student Relationships* (New York: Holt, Rinehart and Winston, 1974).

22. See ibid., chap. 3, for citations of studies listed in Table 6-1.

23. John Douglas, *The Home and the School* (London: MacGibbon and Kee, 1964).

24. Bruce Tuckman and Martin Bierman, "Beyond Pygmalion: Galatea in the Schools" (Paper presented at the annual meeting of the American Educational Research Association, New York: February 1971).

25. J. Palardy, "What Teachers Believe—What Children Achieve," *Elementary School Journal* 69 (1969): 370-374.

26. Brophy and Goode, *Teacher-Student Relationships*, pp. 86-89.

27. Ibid., pp. 93-100.

28. Ibid., pp. 104-105.

29. Jerome T. Murphy and David K. Cohen, "Accountability in Education: The Michigan Experience," *Public Interest* 36 (1974): 53-81.

30. Henry S. Dyer, "Toward Objective Criteria of Professional Accountability in the Schools of New York City," *Phi Delta Kappan* 52 (1970): 206-211. For a description of this approach and other similar ones, see Allan C. Ornstein and Harriet Talmage, "The Promise and Politics of Accountability," *Bulletin of the National Association of Secondary School Principals* 58 (1974): 11-19.

7 The Politics and Rise of Teacher Organizations

T.M. Stinnett and Raymond E. Cleveland

Educators have long closed their eyes to the reality of the American education system. Years ago a small group of people established the procedures and policies and pulled the strings for the educational establishment. But that has long since passed and there exists today, not one group of individuals, but a highly complex matrix of influences which involves the interaction of group interests, school boards, state departments of education, legislative leaders, state and federal courts, opinion leaders in the mass media, and a host of other lesser affectors.

Educators have been described as being naive in their emphasis that schools be kept out of politics and politics be kept out of schools. The term *naive* suggests a condition of deficiency in informed judgment, a lack of general knowledge of a situation. But educators have been and are informed. A more suitable term would be *psychosis*—a condition of the educational system characterized by defective or lost contact with reality. The notion of keeping the school and its teachers separate from politics has been deeply ingrained in the public concept of the school from colonial times until recent years.

Traditionally a basic precept has been that the public school belonged to the people and was accessible, on an equal basis, to every family's children. And keeping the schools out of politics assured this openness to all. Involved was the idea of preserving the school personnel from political appointments, manipulation, and nepotism. The educator was to be exempt from all influences except the power of truth and free to present that truth to children. Although the basic idea has remained firmly implanted in the minds of a large section of the population, there has been a gradual change in attitude in the last decade. The change is evident, first, in the teachers themselves and, then, among extensive contingents of the population. Teachers have been influenced by the successes of certain labor groups who learned from sweatshop experiences that a nonpolitical posture soon becomes one of pleading for social and economic justice (quite often in the face of public indifference and contempt).

What is now being described as a seasoned, moving force in national politics had its genesis in the public's indifference to the needs of teachers and the schools, particularly during World War II. For the first time teachers became acutely aware that education must have support, and that support had to come from government. This new realism spawned a militancy at the heart of which was a clear realization that schools and teachers are, not outside the body politic in a protected environment, but in the nucleus of the political process. Organized labor has long realized that it has to be aggressive and strong politically if it is to forge the legislation required for favorable negotiation of wages and working conditions in general. The educator standing before the public in the posture of a suppliant would not be effective in securing adequate financial support for the schools or for teachers' salaries.

Although politics still has a negative connotation to many people, it is *power*—that is, it is organized and sustained social influence or control exerted by individuals or groups on the decisions and behavior of others. In a free society organized power is applied through the process of politics. Educators have opportunity for power in all their relationships, both personal and professional. Influence can be brought to bear on the opinions and attitudes of family, neighbors, councilmen, school board members, state legislators, and congressmen. The impact that teachers can have upon the political arena is impressive when each member's sphere of influence is considered. The National Education Association alone has approximately 1.5 million members. Assuming that each NEA member possesses a potential zeal for political action, maintains a strong unanimity on public issues, and influences three persons from his community to join him in initiating legislation favorable to education, then there are a total of four votes per member, or about 6,000,000 votes. Or consider the total number of teachers in the United States at all levels (lower and higher education) regardless of their organizational affiliation; the total would be close to 3,000,000. Using the same presumption of persons teachers could influence as stated above, they could conceivably muster a vote of 10 to 12 million. The political scientist would be quick to regard this as a potential power of greatest significance.

Although personal influences are recognized as a viable means of establishing or altering attitudes, the profession cannot reach peak efficiency unless individual efforts are organized into groups that are concentrated and directed toward common goals. Care must be taken to insure that political activity, as well as partisan enterprises, do not fragment teachers' organizations. The public must recognize that the interests and concerns of teachers are not unlike the concerns shared by others whose goals are the promotion of excellence in education. If teachers become fragmented, the ability to maximize their political strength will be lost because of the time and effort required to resolve internal conflicts. If goals cannot be agreed upon by educators, the public may be inclined to follow other groups offering alternate goals and avenues for reaching them.

Society has become a labyrinth of group interaction. The "town hall" concept of democracy is nearing extinction and becoming increasingly difficult to approximate as American culture becomes more complex. Modern democracy is a process of dynamic tensions. There are groups for something; there are groups against something. The question of identifying and aligning the educator's position with the right group is an involved and sometimes costly process. There is no gain in denouncing this condition. It would be well for the profession to accept it as a fact and hasten to work within the system to modify and refine it for the common good. Most organized groups have common interests to promote and defend. As long as their efforts are just and honest, there is nothing unethical about such group pressures. But it is also true that people with malfeasant and factious objectives will also organize and attempt to further their aims. The political connivance of moneyed interests exists and will continue to thrive until put down by the emergence of other groups with courage and muscle enough to meet the challenge.

The emergence of teachers into the political arena has been and will be denounced by certain interests as an unholy combination of people supported by taxpayer's money, conniving to wrest more from the long-suffering public. Voices are constantly raised against teachers, as public servants, having any rights in the political field. Typical of that view is the following editorial entitled "Arrogant Educator":

> NEA—which seems far more interested these days in politicking than teaching—has endorsed 169 candidates; more endorsements are to come. Interestingly, almost all endorsements are Democrats . . .
>
> Politically speaking, NEA is little more than the Democratic Party's educational arm. The fact should alarm Americans of every persuasion, for here is a theoretically non-political, non-partisan organization devoting prestige and resources to the election of partisan candidates. Worse, these are teachers—employees of the taxpaying public—functioning in their capacity as teachers, not as private citizens.
>
> Presumably some of the tax money that Republicans pay goes to the remuneration of teachers. That some of these teachers . . . should go around calling for the defeat of Republicans hardly seems fair. In fact, it seems decidedly arrogant.[1]

Strangely enough, the writer of that editorial chose to overlook an article reported in the press just one month later which said: "The American Medical Association has earmarked funds to help in the reelection of ten members of the House who supported a health bill backed by the AMA."

The late John F. Kennedy eloquently summed up the case for teachers in politics in an address before the 1957 annual meeting of the American Association of School Administrators:

> It is disheartening to me, and I think alarming to our Republic, to realize how poorly the political profession is regarded in America . . . Unfortunately, this disdain . . . is not only shared by but intensified by the educational profession . . . This disdain for the political profession in our schools did not matter quite as much in the days when active participation in the political affairs of the nation was limited to a select few. But today the implications of national policy necessarily make politicians of us all . . .[2]

More recently Ralph Kimbrough emphasized the same point when he observed:

In past years many educators were enamored with the idea that education should not be in politics . . . [But] studies . . . of power structures have demonstrated that education is—and indeed ought to be—in politics . . . Through the interaction of influentials with each other, and with other leaders and politically active citizens, important channels of communication crystallize . . .

Political action must be based on commitment to attainable legislative goals . . . Every great movement in education has been based upon some purposeful goals that captivated the minds of those who led the movement . . . There are limits to how much educators can improve schooling unless attention and power are focused upon improving the political power system in which the schools function . . .State leaders must be effective (strong) enough to motivate and assist local educators to bring about changes . . . Local leaders need to "stand and be counted" when political strength is needed, in the state education agency.[3]

Stephen Bailey and his associates state bluntly the thesis of their book, *Schoolmen and Politics:*

This study is built around a very simple proposition. The amount of money state governments make available for general aid to public schools is determined politically . . . The nature of the formulae and the amounts spent under them are products of political conflict and resolution. If state aid to education is to continue at its present rate, or is to expand, it will be because politically active schoolmen have the knowledge and skill to marshal effective political power.[4]

To be independent of organized power in American society is idealistic. The individual who does not wish to actively participate in politics is not free of its pressures. He or she is consistently the object of overt and covert influences. The educator, again, must face reality, align himself with honorable power structures, and apologize to no one for doing so. Educational power, like all other political groups, must be judged in terms of its objectives. The teaching profession must never lose sight of its ultimate goal of improving the school program—to do everything possible to optimize the learning situation and improve the quality of the educational experience.

Political power, if it reflects a true opinion of a broadly based group and if it is accountable, is inherently ethical. The generalizations and ideas endorsed by the represented group must be concrete to the degree that they may serve as a "modus operandi" to the leaders of the group. Not every member of the body at large can vote, and the leaders must have a dynamic avenue for communications to the people represented. The education "establishment"—NEA, AFT, AASA, and AAUP[a]—have broad and deep commitments to social and educational objectives. From the classroom, however, these representative groups, because of

[a]National Education Association, American Federation of Teachers, American Association of School Administrators, and American Association of University Professors.

their size and complex organizations, seem at times to be representing a relatively small segment of the teaching profession. As the process of politics and group power is accepted as a standard order of procedure instead of a clandestine activity, the personnel who constitute grass-roots professional education are destined to become more valuable. They will offer a new view with depth and breadth because of their experiences and diversity.

A new power relationship, based upon the political realities of a free society, is manifesting itself. The public acceptance of this virile relationship between political and educational forces gives promise that quality education for all will be the foundation of the educational policy of every state. And the time seems to be at hand when groups of professional educators should coalesce and form powerful and effective agencies for influencing political decisions. It is time to take a rational, realistic approach to the future of the profession and present a united front. There are some precautions, however, which teacher organizations must observe:

1. Teachers' political activity should never be exercised through the children they teach; nor should parents be involved directly.
2. The seeking of power–personal power–is dangerous. Each organization must establish its own restraints.
3. The public good must be of paramount concern, both in school legislation and in governmental actions.
4. Teachers' organizations must concern themselves with far broader concerns than those pursued by educational organizations. Teachers cannot, of course, carry the whole load. But they can exert tremendous power to keep government honest and other pressure groups within reasonable limits. The latter is especially true regarding the unorganized, who are subject to exploitation, mistreatment, and the worst kind of injustices, unless there is balanced power to check the offenders.
5. Teachers' organizations must be broad in their support of issues and persons. There must be opportunity for all members to participate in decision making. The worst possible situation for teachers engaging in political action would result from a few selected individuals dominating their organization(s).

Teachers must shed the persisting naiveté about politics and engage vigorously in its processes. No instrument of government is more involved in politics than public schools. In this connection, the membership of the teaching profession is changing. Teachers are younger; they are young enough to know that they must do for themselves what their predecessors depended upon public benevolence to do for them. Other professions learned this lesson long ago. The present corps of teachers know that they must seek legislation that will, as is true of most other professions, put the power in the group to determine its own destiny through self-governance. The educator has a choice between initiating change or accepting the decisions of the outsider. The following is an account of teachers' influence in the 1974 general election:

> America's school teachers emerged [in the 1974 general election] as a potent new force in national politics.
>
> The teachers claimed that an impressive 80 percent of the congressional candidates they endorsed and financed had won election.
>
> The teachers are already making plans for 1976, to play a key role in the election of the next President.
>
> Abandoning its former hands-off attitude toward politics, the NEA this year got involved in 310 House and Senate races.
>
> One goal is an increase in federal education aid. The U.S. now pays about 8 percent of education costs and the NEA wants the federal share upped to 33 percent.
>
> The other goal is the passage of pending legislation which would extend to teachers the protection of the National Labor Relations Act and guarantee certain bargaining rights to teachers in contract negotiations with local school boards.[5]

Rise of Teachers' Organizations

The chief means of the teaching profession to exert political influence is through strong professional organizations. The first criterion of a recognized profession is generally held to be a comprehensive professional association to which its members, or a majority of them, belong. For the lawyer, for example, it would be the American Bar Association; for the physician, the American Medical Association; for the dentist the American Dental Association. And for virtually all professionals, there are also state and local associations. Sometimes the practitioner belongs to these and not to the national organizations.

Teaching probably has more professional associations than any other profession; the Education Directory lists over 1,200.[6] One reason for the proliferation of teacher organizations is that membership generally is voluntary. In Canada, on the other hand, the law requires that practicing teachers in the public schools be members of their provincial (state) teachers' association. Another reason for the amount of American teachers associations is the large number of specialties in teaching–science, mathematics, and so on–with each specialty having one or more associations, at both the national and state levels.

For teachers in elementary and secondary schools there are two major professional associations–the National Education Association (NEA) and the American Federation of Teachers (AFT). There is at least one NEA affiliate in each state, which is a comprehensive organization to which teachers, administrators, and special service personnel belong. And, there are nearly 500 statewide NEA associations, most of which serve special interests of teachers, such as an association of English Teachers or of science teachers. In addition, there are thousands of local associations. Since there are about 16,000 local school districts in the United States, it can be assumed that there is a local education association in most of those districts.

Both the NEA and AFT had their aeges in political situations which will be described in the following sections. In the case of the AFT it is clear and unequivocal that its beginning stemmed from the need for political action. In the case of the NEA, while the intentions of origin were not so clear, political factors were considered.

National Education Association

The NEA came into being as the result of the demands of a group of state education associations. The first such professional organizations in the United States were organized to promote the public schools, among which were the Pennsylvania Society for the Promotion of Public Schools, Western Literary Institute and College of Professional Teachers, Lyceum, and American Association for the Advancement of Education.[7] The first real teachers association, the Society of Associated Teachers, was founded in 1794 in New York City. By 1840, when the development of state school systems was well underway, state education associations began to be formed. The first states to found permanent education associations were Connecticut, Massachusetts, and Rhode Island, in 1845. By 1856 some seventeen states had formed associations as comprehensive, general organizations. In 1857 the presidents of ten of the state education associations issued an invitation to their colleagues in other states to meet in Philadelphia on 15 May 1857 and form the National Teachers Association. In 1870 the first two departments, the National Association of Superintendents (now AASA) and the American Normal School Association (now AACTE)[b] joined with the National Teachers Association to form the National Education Association. In 1906 the Congress chartered this association as the National Education Association of the United States. There were only forty-three members in its formative year, but by 1974 the NEA had about 1.5 million members. The membership figures of the NEA are a good index of its growth; these are contained in Table 7-1.

Why was there a demand for this national association? Because of the success the state associations had had in influencing the growth of the public schools in their respective states. The invitation to form the new association did not mention politics or political action, but it did believe "that what has been done for states by state associations may be done for the whole country by a National Association . . ." This would seem to imply that a national association was needed to press the goal of a well-rounded, well-financed system of free public schools throughout the United States. Not until 1866 could women be members

[b]American Association of Colleges of Teacher Education.

Table 7-1
Membership Figures of the NEA by Decades

Year	Membership
1857	43
1870	170
1880	354
1890	5,474
1900	2,332
1910	6,909
1920	22,850
1930	216,188
1940	203,429
1950	453,797
1960	713,994
1970	1,100,000

of the new association or vote. Men continued to dominate the NEA until the decade 1910-1920, when teachers led a revolt that reorganized the national body and began pressing for federal legislation to aid the public schools. A legislative commission was created, and teachers began insisting upon concerted efforts to improve their general conditions as professional workers.

William Russell, one of the nation's best-known educators, at the first meeting proposed that the national organization become the focus of making teaching into a profession. He proposed that teachers themselves pass upon the qualifications of those admitted to practice. His proposal was that admission to memberships would serve as legal evidence (certification) of competence to teach. While Russell's proposal was never adopted as he proposed it, NEA in time did, through its state affiliates, organize to propose the requirements for certification and the standards for accreditation of institutions preparing teachers.

The National Teachers Association and its successor, the National Education Association, addressed themselves to a great range of problems and were instrumental in solving many of them. There was, for example, the need for expansion of institutions to prepare teachers, first the state normal school and later the state teachers colleges, plus public and private colleges and universities. It has been estimated that by 1900 perhaps as many as 300 normal schools or normal training classes in high schools and academies existed throughout the country.

Another problem was teachers' salaries. In 1857 the average salary for male teachers was $24 per month and for women, $16.65 per month for a four- or five-month school year. In 1973-74 average salaries for a school year for elementary school teachers was about $9,000 and for high school teachers, about $10,000. Lengthening the school term was another tough problem that the new association undertook until the length of the school year became a standard nine-month term. The establishment of state retirement systems for teachers was another achievement of the associations. The long, hard, and bitter fight to secure federal assistance in supporting the public school finally came to a measure of fruition in 1965 with the passage of the Elementary and Secondary Education Act.

Beginning in the early 1950s, the AFT began a massive thrust to organize teachers, especially in the large cities, and has enjoyed some spectacular successes. This drive has forced the NEA to restructure its organization and to overhaul its policies. For example, in 1968, the NEA consisted of eighty-six units, including seventeen headquarters divisions, thirty-four departments, and thirty-five committees and commissions. By 1973-74, because of policy and organizational changes in the NEA, the number of units has reduced to twenty-seven and the number of departments has declined to three. The units, especially the departments, which have disaffiliated themselves from NEA resulted from either (1) their opposition to the use of "labor tactics" by NEA or (2) the domination of classroom teachers under the new structure. School board members and all types of administrators are vigorously, often bitterly, opposed to dividing the profession into irreconcilable elements that result from collective bargaining or professional negotiation.

American Federation of Teachers

While political activity was not clearly a material factor in the founding of the NEA, such is not the case in regard to the founding of the AFT. Indeed, political considerations were the direct and unquestioned cause of the formation of this organization. Moreover, teachers urged its formation and its political aspects and sought membership affiliation with it and organized labor. Teachers, looking for help in a desperate situation in Chicago, could find only one ally—the American Federation of Labor (AFL).

In 1899 Chicago teachers had not had a pay raise in twenty years. Elementary school teachers, for example, were paid $500 a year; maximum salary after eleven years of service was $800. The Chicago School Board treated the teachers' requests for increases with contempt. The NEA was of no help. It did not at that time have the machinery, know-how, or will to try to rectify the situation. The teachers decided to help themselves and began by organizing the Chicago Teachers Federation to investigate the causes of the situation. At the time there was no affiliation with labor, nor apparently any intention of such. The federation was able to influence the board to raise the maximum salary to $1,000 a year. But after a year the board rescinded the action because, it said, it did not have the money for the raise.

The Chicago teachers refused to accept the board's retrenchment and were determined to find out why the board did not have money for the modest pay raise they had requested. The results of the federation's study showed that a number of large businesses, including public utilities, were not being assessed for property taxes and were therefore not paying taxes. Apparently, this situation had existed for a number of years. Although there were laws requiring the assessing of such property, the responsible public officials were catering to the wealth of the corporations by ignoring those laws. The teachers donated money to a fund to seek a mandamus ruling from the courts to enforce the law. Their suit was successful, resulting in about $600,000 additional tax money each year, about a third of which went to the schools. But the teachers received no pay raise, and in 1902 the board actually reduced teachers' salaries.

The Chicago Federation of Teachers made many appeals to the NEA for help in their local situation. But help never came. And when salaries were reduced in 1920 they affiliated with the AFL. Between 1902 and 1916, some twenty federations in ten states were formed and affiliated with the AFL. In 1915, goaded by criticism from business groups about teachers joining unions, the Chicago school board adopted the Loeb Rule (Loeb was president of the Chicago School Board), which prohibited teachers from belonging to labor unions. The teachers, aided by the Chicago Federation of Labor, were able to secure a temporary injunction against the Loeb Rule; the injunction was later made permanent by the courts. The board, angered by this action, retaliated by firing sixty-eight teachers who belonged to the labor organization. Turning to the AFL for help again in 1917, the teachers were able to persuade the Illinois legislature to abolish the existing school board and establish a new one under a new code of education laws.

In June 1915 an invitation was sent to all teachers' federations to meet and form a national federation. The following group of federations became the founders of the AFT in April of 1916: The Chicago Federation of Teachers, the Chicago Federation of Men Teachers, the Gary (Indiana) Teachers Federation, the Teachers Union of the City of New York, the Oklahoma Teachers Federation, the Scranton (Pennsylvania) Teachers Association, and the High School Teachers Union of Washington, D.C. Goals for the AFT were spelled out in its constitution: (1) to bring associations of teachers into mutual assistance and cooperation; (2) to secure for teachers all rights to which they are entitled; (3) to raise the standards of the teaching profession by securing conditions essential to good teaching; and (4) to promote such democratization of schools as will enable them to equip their pupils to take their places in the industrial, social, and political life of the community.

The AFT has consistently claimed to be a classroom teachers organization, while NEA has always been a general, or all-inclusive, membership association. Until AFT amended its constitution in 1966 to exclude administrators from the principal up, they had been permitted to belong. AFT consists of state federations in most states and about 1,900 local federations. Table 7-2 shows AFT membership from its inception in 1918 to 1970.

Teachers Organizations and The Future

What will happen in the competitive battle between the NEA and AFT is difficult to predict. There are too many variables and unknowns involved. Will the organizations merge, for example? There have been concerted efforts toward this end. But NEA has broken off negotiations, refusing merger if it means its members have to affiliate with organized labor:

> NEA President Catherine Garrett, in speaking in opposition to the merger said: Our proposal sets forth three basic requirements we would insist upon for a merger. . . . First, the new organization must be free to take its own positions and pursue its own objectives . . . Our proposal provides that the organization would not be affiliated with AFL-CIO. Second, NEA commitment to the rights of minorities must be preserved—that minority representation must reflect at least the minority population of the organization. And third, . . . that such a guarantee is best found in the secret ballot and our proposal mandates secret ballots in the selection of officers and making changes in the governance document of its new organization.[8]

The question of which national teachers organization will become predominant in the future is complicated because both the NEA and AFT are backing proposed bills in Congress to declare the rights of teachers in all states to collective bargaining and to strike. If these bills become law, they would eventually cover all but a few public employees, such as perhaps policemen or firemen. Such laws could be disastrous for many government workers and for the public. In some states, close to 20 percent of all workers are employees of the various governmental units.

Table 7-2
AFT Membership since 1918 by Decades

Year	Membership
1918	1,500
1920	10,000
1930	7,000
1940	30,000
1950	41,000
1960	59,000
1970	205,000

Both the NEA and AFT in lobbying for their bills point to Executive Order 10.988, which provides public workers with certain rights that ought to belong to all workers. The American Association of Municipal, County, and State Employees, one of the largest unions in the United States is an out-growth of Executive Order 10.988, which specifies the right of federal employees to negotiate but not to strike. Albert Shanker, president of the AFT, rose to power in New York City by leading the members of his union in several strikes. He has hopes of eventually organizing the more than 3,000,000 public school and college teachers into the largest union in the United States.

The NEA has only recently entered the field of direct political action by establishing the Political Action Committee. The NEA claims to have been influential in the November 1974 national elections in electing four of every five candidates backed by the PAC: PAC-supported candidates won in 229 of 282 House election contests and were successful in twenty-one of twenty-eight Senate races. The NEA endorsed 310 federal office seekers in forty-eight states. A total of 165 candidates in forty-four states received financial aid (from contributions of members of the Political Action Committee) amounting to $225,000. State and local associations, affiliated with NEA contributed $25 million to federal, state, and local races.

The AFT plans to appoint a new head of its Committee for Political Action (COPE). And Shanker, predicted that COPE's annual income would eventually amount to an excess of $1 million. Hence, the battle lines are drawn. The NEA and AFT will fight with political power, until merger does occur or one of the organizations goes under.

Notes

1. *Dallas Morning News*, 12 August 1974, p. 2-D.

2. *Schools on the Threshold of a New Era*, Official Report of the American Association of School Administrators, Washington, D.C., 1957, pp. 158-159.

3. Ralph B. Kimbrough, "Power Structures and Education Change," in *Planning and Effecting Needed Changes in Education*, ed. Edgar L. Morphet and Charles O. Ryan (New York: Citation Press, 1967), p. 115.

4. Stephen K. Bailey et al., *Schoolmen and Politics* (Syracuse, N.Y.: Syracuse University Press, 1962), p. vii.

5. Richard J. Maloy, "School Teachers Emerge as Potent New Force," *Lafayette, Louisiana Advertiser*, 10 November 1974, p. 12.

6. U.S. Office of Education, Department of Health, Education and Welfare, *Education Directory 1973* (Washington, D.C.: U.S. Government Printing Office, 1973).

7. R. Freeman Butts and Lawrence A. Cremin, *A History of Education in American Culture* (New York: Holt, Rinehart and Winston, 1953).

8. Catherine Garrett, "Report of the President of the Proceedings of the NEA Representative Assembly," NEA, Washington, D.C., 1973, pp. 10-11.

8 New Entry Requirements and New Programs for College Students

Martin Haberman

Changes are not accepted with neutral responses. A normative valence of better or worse is inevitably attached to any change. New college entrance requirements, such as equivalency examinations in place of high school attendance, will inevitably be understood as a change that either improves or erodes the existing standards. Does a youth incarcerated at fourteen, a military veteran, an upward-bound student, and an adult housewife, all of whom "test out," present an equivalent background for college admission when compared to typical high school graduates?

Those faculty, administrators, students, and laymen who believe in everyone's "right" to higher education will tend to attach positive values (for example, increased relevance, more responsive institutions, equalizing educational opportunity) to colleges and universities that adopt new entrance requirements. Those who believe in the intrinsic worth of the traditional curricula will suspect the new entry requirements of watering down, lowering, and eroding the standards.

Similar reactions are to be expected to the adoption of new programs. Changes are not accepted as merely added complexities to be understood with detached neutrality. Those who, for a variety of reasons, seek change will be prone to attach positive values to new programs; those who seek to preserve existing patterns will be likely to attribute negative values to new programs. It has become commonplace for any new idea—whether an admissions policy or a program innovation—to justify its difference by somehow proving it is not a diminution of the existing standards. This is usually accomplished by the device of "adding on" rather than replacing. New admissions policies are added to old ones so that several sets may be invoked simultaneously. New courses are added so that they coexist with the old. Thus academic peace is negotiated among the movers and shakers, on the one hand, and the preservers, on the other. In effect, little is dropped but much is added, so that faculty and students (and particularly faculty) can do what they choose. This negotiated truce, however, does not prevent some from feeling that new and different entrance requirements are indeed "lower," while others are convinced that new standards are vital for higher education to prove that it has some redeeming social significance.

Of all the innovations being bandied about in higher education, none bears the potential for greater radical change than the *external degree.* Essentially, the external degree is one that does not include or require residential study in a particular place. This negative definition of what the degree is *not* leaves open a variety of instructional processes which may be utilized by those working toward an external degree: correspondence courses; newspaper courses; off-campus courses; television and radio courses; independent field work and research; work-study programs; travel; telephone seminars; and, most of all, the notion of awarding college credit for prior life experiences.

While it is not incumbent on an external degree program to award credit for prior life experiences, the basic assumptions are that (1) learning should not be confined to a place (that is, to an institution with scholars and a library) and (2) learning is continuous and occurs before, during, and after a period of matriculation. These assumptions have made it typical for prior life learning credits to be awarded in external degree programs. But whether the degree program is some residential innovation or an external degree, the practice of awarding students credit for what they have learned through experiences prior to college admission raises many questions—all of which relate to the standards of higher education.

There are at least fifteen major issues that must be dealt with before colleges can credit prior life experiences. Dealing with these issues involves conceptualizing their pros and cons in order to raise the debate to intellectual discourse and beyond the unreflective, traditional responses. Naturally, many of the issues cannot be so easily supported or refuted; the presentation is admittedly an extreme one and is intended to be a stimulant to analysis. Similarly, the fifteen issues presented here are neither exhaustive nor mutually exclusive. Many others pertain and are inextricably interrelated.

The basic assumption of this chapter is that no institution should initiate or reject a program of crediting prior life experiences without having at least considered the issues and obtained tentative answers. In essence, the issues are a response to the question, What policies and practices must a particular institution take before launching (or even considering) a prior life credit option? Each issue is discussed cursorily for purposes of exposition and is not analyzed to the depth that program planners should pursue in developing real programs.

Should Credit Be Awarded for Particular Experiences or for Quality of Performance in Those Experiences?

The practice of awarding all World War II veterans with honorable discharges six college credits is the most notable example of assuming that a particular set of life experiences is inevitably salutary and of equal value for all. If this approach has merit, then parents of *x* number of children should receive a standard number of credits. Similarly, parolees with *x* years in prison; workers with *x* years of work experience; travelers with *x* years "on the road"; indeed, people with *x* years of living can be awarded a fixed amount of college credit. The assumption is that some experiences hold such potent educative power that it can be assumed that all who have undergone the experience will be changed and enlightened in some manner and to an equal degree.

The opposite view asserts that experiences are not in themselves inherently educative but must exert some demonstrably positive influences on the individuals who experience them. This means that a quality dimension is required: How well should an individual perform in a particular life activity in order to receive credit?

This issue presents two extremes. The first assumes that some life experiences are of greater significance than others and awards credit for living through such milestone experiences. The second assumes that there must be standards for judging how well individuals have performed in particular life situations.

Should Credit Be Awarded for Current Demonstrations of Competency or for Documentation of Performance in Previous Life Situations?

Common practice is to test a student's abilities in some manner at the time he or she seeks to receive college credit. The assumptions made are that (1) learning, if truly accomplished, will be retained from some previous time; and (2) means of assessing learning in colleges are not significantly different from how those learnings might be assessed if they were judged at the time the students actually participated in the particular experiences. This approach is compatible with the tradition in many colleges and universities that permit students to test out of courses for many years.

The opposite view is that the educative values gained from participating in particular life experiences cannot be assessed by a written test, in an interview, or by a simulated performance. Students are given the responsibility of documenting the quality of their learnings and performances in prior life situations. Portfolios of students' self-reports, letters of reference, artifacts, awards and witnesses' statements are accumulated to attest to the quality of their performances. Whether the test-out or the portfolio approach is used, there is still the enormous problem of designating some minimum level, or standard of goodness, that will make a particular life experience creditable.

Should Credit Be Awarded for Learning Subject Matter Represented in Higher Education or Also for Learning Not Represented in the Curricula?

If a college offers a course in american history, introductory botany, german literature of the nineteenth century, swimming, marriage and the family, and so forth, the students can demonstrate that they already know the material and receive credit. In this approach, the college or university is quite open about the conditions and processes by which the student may have learned the material, but quite firm about retaining the notion of translating the student's experiences into existing and accepted college syllabi. The students bear the responsibility for adapting everything they have learned in life into the way the subjects are taught in the college. Learning in areas, subject matters, and fields of inquiry not taught in the university cannot be credited; if there are no comparable courses, no course numbers, and no amount of credits, then how can a student's knowledge be entered on the transcript?

The opposite position assumes that (1) subject matters not represented in existing college curricula may be as worthy as those that are (for example, ESP may be as educative as studying learning in rats and Yiddish may be as educative as German); and (2) learning gained through life experiences need not be translated into existing college syllabi. For example, a chef should not be given a nutrition test and a grounds keeper should not have to take a botany exam in order for them to transform and translate their knowledge into the shapes required by the university.

Should Learning be Credited by Separate Disciplines and University Departments or in the Integrated Forms in which They Are Acquired in Life Experiences?

Higher education has a history of trying to integrate studies across disciplines. While there have been notable successes in which actual social and physical problems have been identified and then studied in multidisciplinary ways, it is still quite common to find fractionated general education programs. Students are traditionally offered discrete, introductory courses. The integration of the studies and their application to real-life problems are typically considered the students' responsibility. It is natural, therefore, to expect that many institutions that become involved in crediting prior life learnings will approach the task by examining hunks of living (child-rearing, occupational experiences, avocational pursuits, and so on) and then break them down (for example, three credits of child development, three credits of business management, three credits of painting). Those in favor of this approach argue that for purposes of analysis and study it is quite legitimate and desirable for the separate disciplines to continue to make distinctive analyses of what appears to be a general problem area.

The opposite view argues that life should not follow and be made to fit college studies but, rather, that all education should be preparation for living—and problems of living do not present themselves in neat segments. Why is it important to label one piece of student knowledge as a political science concept, another as an economic concept, and a third concept as falling between several disciplines? This position advocates that colleges describe students' learning achievements in ways that reflect what they actually know—even if this requires new categorizations of knowledge or strange statements on college transcripts.

Should Credit Represent Systematic Study that Can be Logically Structured or Be Awarded for Learning Derived from Uncontrolled, Random Situations of Living?

If learning generally proceeds from elementary ideas to advanced concepts and if experts exist in all fields who can sequence the teaching of the disciplines, then students cannot be ready to benefit from advanced studies unless they have had the prerequisites. Proponents of this view assume that sound learning is logically organized. The opposing position is that learning is psychologically organized: learning increases in response to students' interests, past experiences, and motivations. Numerous examples are cited of students who have learned advanced concepts without prerequisites or before having had elementary courses.

Those who believe that learning must be logically sequenced will likely regard learning that results from experience as random and disorganized. Those who believe that individual students inevitably place their own psychological organization on what they know will likely regard crediting life experiences as feasible. Those who believe in sequential learning will argue that graduate schools will expect students to have proceeded through structured training. Those who believe in psychological learning will argue that even the most advanced graduate training can occur in the same way as learning that was derived from life experience.

Should Credit Be Awarded for Study with Scholars and Peers or for Independent, Self-Selected Activities?

On the issue of formal versus informal instruction, there is much experience to support the belief that students learn much, not only from teachers but also from peers. The sharing of ideas, the cognitive analysis with others regarding common problems, and the give and take of criticism have all become a basic part of higher education. Even advanced students doing research theses are prone to remark favorably about the values of peers or a critical but knowledgeable professor. Obviously, there will be many life experiences that have not taken place under these optimum conditions. That people may have been left to their own resources during many of their life experiences will be considered a significant reason for not granting college credit.

Those who would credit life experiences recognize the post hoc nature of the practice. They realize they are extracting and identifying learning from life experiences which they did not pursue, at the time, for their potential learning values. They also realize they were not formally engaged with peers in the analysis of what was happening to them. Frequently, however, students can recall friends, relatives, coworkers, and others who helped to clarify their life experiences. They argue that few, if any, of their life experiences were ever experienced in solitary confinement; while they did not regard peers as costudents and teachers, there were always others with whom they interacted and who may have been unwitting but highly effective instructors. Some even argue that during their life experiences they received formal instruction from religious advisors, psychiatrists, marriage counselors, physicians, lawyers, architects, accountants, and the like.

Should Credit Involve Required Reading in a Good Library or be Awarded for Knowledge Gained without Required Reading?

Not only those who believe in a curriculum comprised of the 100 great books, but also many (most?) college faculty are convinced of the necessity for intensive library work. Extension and off-campus courses are still regarded with suspicion by faculty who question the lack of student access to ample academic library facilities as a concession of quality to convenience. The notion of crediting life experiences after they have occurred, so that students could not have possibly engaged in any systematic reading during their experiences, is viewed as an insurmountable deficiency. It is one thing to regard life experiences as potentially equal to reading and thereby a means of gaining contact with the experiences of all mankind. It is quite another to completely disregard the value of reading experiences.

Those who believe that life experiences can be credited argue that much varied reading is likely to occur in conjunction with many experiences (novels, periodicals, newspapers, and so on) and that other media, such as motion pictures, television, and radio, will also supplement almost all life experiences.

These proponents argue that the issue is really between those who would prescribe what should be read and those who would have faith in materials that are self-selected. Are members of book clubs who read the biographies of blacks, women, and American Indians gaining a less academic view of American history than those who took formal courses and read only the biographies of Benjamin Franklin and other white males?

Should Credit Reflect the Time Devoted to Study or the Learning Achieved?

Although the Carnegie unit has dominated secondary and higher education for more than half a century, many academics see value in using "time spent" as a basis for determining credit. Class hours plus hours in independent study are still used to determine the number of credits attached to a particular course. It is almost as if professors believed in the intrinsic value of the experience of attending their classes. This would, in a very real sense, be similar to believing in the intrinsic value attached to the experiences of military service or marriage or anything else.

Many faculty support the notion of connecting time spent with credit by citing learning theories. Some skills require short practice periods over a length of time. Value changes require time. Learning abstract concepts requires numerous examples and variations about which to generalize. The actual learning of students is offered as the rationale for connecting more time with more credit.

Those who would credit life experiences argue that frequently students spend years in activities that receive only a few credits. Some point to the irrelevancy of effort (that is, the time spent) and emphasize that the learning gained is all that really matters. A few proponents, such as those of one university in New York, actually agree that time is important—even more important than credit—and award students years and months of college time toward a four-year degree, rather than any number of college credits. In essence, it is understandable that a college system based on credits awarded by time expended *and* demonstrated knowledge would be reluctant to look at only the knowledge gained. Faculty would become mere testers if there were no values attached to attending classes. Interaction with faculty surely goes beyond the knowledge gained. All teachers would like to believe that the knowledge they tested for was only a small sample of an infinitely broader universe of knowledge that the student has gained in their classes. The life experience proponents are, in effect, asking faculty to consider that they may be unnecessary to students with appropriate life experiences. This author believes that time is a more critical dimension for life experience students than for typical college students since valuable life experiences are lengthy and depend on self-discovery as well as upon informal teachers.

Should Credit Represent Some System in which Students Are Compared with Other Students Be Conceived of as a Noncomparative, Noncompetitive Form of Self-Development?

In most institutions of higher education, standards are relative. Even where there are criterion standards, comparative judgments inevitably influence the grades awarded, the faculty assessments, and the students' self-evaluations. The notions of the distinguished student, the "Gentleman C," the failure, and so on, are concepts derived from comparisons. In some cases these are formal ("We mark on a curve"). In other cases the comparisons exist in the subjective responses of faculty and students. Such comparisons are considered by many as "the American way." Not only are the standards considered sound if students are compared, but also the whole process is sanctified as appropriate preparation for subsequent life in a competitive adult society. High standards are usually interpreted by faculty to mean, not that more is taught and learned, but that more students are unfavorably judged in comparison to others.

Clearly, crediting life experiences means not being able to take advantage of the benefits of comparative, competitive study. While some life experiences may have involved competition, others may not. It is possible that individuals who have never tried to compete and others who have tried but lost will seek to have their life experiences credited. The goal of life experience credit is developmental; growth is determined in terms of the degree and nature of the individual's changes in relation to himself or herself. Since life experiences are never identical but are characterized by great diversity, the learning that accrues can best be understood in terms of their meaning for the individual involved. While it is true that common experiences can be extracted from different life experiences and then tested for, just as minimum standards can be assessed in college classes, the thrust of crediting life experiences is to credit personalized learning rather than common experiences.

Should Credit Be Awarded for Supervised Study or for Self-determined Activities?

The trend in the last several decades has been toward an increasing number of electives and student choices. And students have been offered increasing options within courses regarding their assignments, their readings, and the nature of their evaluation. There remains, nevertheless, some degree of faculty control. Most institutions still have a set of requirements for graduation and a senior summary as a final warning system to would-be graduates. Most institutions still have departments that specify what constitutes a major or specialization and the prerequisites and requirements that may be involved in such study. In effect, most faculty and most institutions feel some measure of responsibility for controlling the studies made available to students. The motivation for this supervision is a need, not always to merely dominate students, but to exert some measure of quality control over the institution's products. There is a factor of accountability and responsibility built into this system. Remarks such as, "We can't permit this student to become a graduate of Siwash Tech" are typical. There is a feeling akin to a craftsman's pride that a particular faculty often shares as a common value. Students are considered both as learners and a reflection of the faculty's competence.

Crediting life experience is, on the other hand, an open, self-selected curriculum that is unsupervised. The faculty, in effect, has exerted no controls over the learning and bears no direct responsibility for it. A student may have learned concepts equivalent to those offered in an introductory psychology course, but he may have learned them while engaged in "illegal" activities—activities in which his learning transcended the typical college course in depth and in style. It has become common to hear faculty say that their particular college provides a polish, a sophistication that goes beyond the stated curriculum and stamps a graduate as one of their alumni. The life experience faculty, however, while responsible for identifying their students' learning, can in no way be held accountable for them.

Should Credit Be Awarded Only by Faculty or by Evaluators Acting on Behalf of Faculty?

Next to approving dissertations, the single most important responsibility of the faculty in present college programs is to award credit. This responsibility has evolved into a faculty right. Faculty approval is necessary to extend this right to new faculty, to adjunct faculty, and to graduate faculty. The basic assumption is that faculty have exclusive control over the subject matters for which students are granted credit. Students do not grant themselves or each other credit; faculty in one department or college do not grant credit in another. Faculty status carries the right to define what activities should be credit bearing and to award specific students a specific number of credits. If there is any power involved in being a faculty member, it is concentrated in this capability for awarding credit.

Proponents of crediting life experiences sometimes involve regular faculty; at other times personnel who are faculty surrogates test students or evaluate them in other ways before awarding credit. This means, in effect, that the ultimate decisions (that is, awarding of credit) and frequently large blocks of credit for admittedly unusual forms of learning, are made by nonfaculty personnel. In the educational hierarchy these people are often considered to be lower status. As a result, standards in life experience programs are sometimes considered to be low.

Advocates of life experience programs argue that special expertise is involved in evaluating students' life experiences, that such evaluations take more time than faculty members can devote, and that subject matters are often interdisciplinary or beyond faculty specialization. Frequently this issue involves more than a value difference since there are administrative policies or even state statutes that regulate who may award credit. In some programs a faculty member serves as a figurehead while nonfaculty staff actually evaluate students' learning and award the credit for their life experiences.

Should Credit Be Awarded for Professional-Technical-Vocational Competencies or for General Education?

It is inevitable that most life learnings should be assumed to derive from occupational activities rather than from other forms of life experience. As a consequence, the learning offered for evaluation will be heavily weighted in terms of job skills, careers, technical competencies, and professions that individuals have performed without college degrees. It will be easiest for college programs to credit such vocational competencies: faculty will be less threatened since they will not be experts in these areas; critics will be less numerous since colleges do not usually have experts in a wide range of specific occupations; and students will perceive these as the areas in which they have worked hardest and should receive credit.

If credit is granted for professional-technical-vocational competencies, then students will be expected to pursue liberal studies during their subsequent on-campus or formal studies. Since most degrees are in the arts and sciences, serious questions will be raised about a degree program in which credit for occupational experiences is followed by general education.

Other proponents of crediting life experience take a broader view. They seek to help students extract learning from the fullest possible range of their life experiences. In this way, the prior life credits awarded are not primarily for work experiences but are, rather, in areas of general education. While this is a greater threat to faculty, since they also offer general education courses, there is a logical opportunity for students to build on this general education and to specialize later in their subsequent studies. An arts and science degree is also more appropriate for students awarded large blocks of credit in general education rather than in vocational studies.

There is no question that awarding credits for vocational-technical learning will be more politically safe and more easily evaluated. Awarding credit for general education will be more difficult but more appropriate, given the nature of people's actual life experiences.

Should Credit for Prior Learning Be Awarded and Recorded in the Usual Forms of Credits and Hours or Awarded and Transcribed in New Forms?

The traditional argument is that life experiences should be translated into college credits because the degree is an end in itself. The opposite view is that college study is merely an instrumentality for living the examined life. If individuals demonstrate they have already lived the examined life why is it necessary to transform real experience into credits? Arguments for translating real experience into typical forms of college credit also include pragmatic notions: employers and graduate admissions officers can only interpret traditional transcripts; those who compute grade point averages need a conventional transcript; computers are programmed to print college credits in specific ways.

Proponents of new transcript forms argue that honesty compels narrative statements for describing the learnings achieved in life experiences. They maintain that admissions officers and registrars should be expeditors not overseers. Students receiving credit for life experiences seem quite eager to have their experiences described in summary form on their transcripts. Because higher education institutions are frequently large organizations, the issue involves the efficient mass production of transcripts versus the more expensive and difficult personalized account of accomplishments.

Should Credit Be Awarded Apart from Students' Entrance into a Particular Program or as Part of Students' Plans for Completion of a Total Program?

Advocates of awarding credit apart from entrance into a study program take the position that life learnings can be assessed by testing out or in a relatively brief period. They also believe that students are entitled to the credit they have earned whether they wish to matriculate for a degree, take a few additional courses, or engage in no further study. Learning is learning; if the students have achieved, they should be credited.

Proponents of the opposing view argue that assessing students' learning is a lengthy, complex experience which can only transpire over a period of several months. Further, the institutional investment in evaluating students' life experiences should only be a precursor to their subsequent study. (No tuition is charged for prior life credits awarded to students, although in some cases a nominal examination fee may be assessed.) Finally, those who advocate that students complete a total program argue that colleges should have specific programs planned for various student groups and that recruiting students to merely credit their prior life learnings is an incomplete, unnecessary activity. In an extreme form it might be possible to state the issue as a choice between crediting students' experiences as an initial entrance assessment versus the withholding of all credit for prior life experiences until the student has completed all degree requirements.

Should Credit Be Awarded to Any College Student for Life Experiences or Be Reserved for Particular Students?

Those who argue that all students may be entitled to credit for prior life learnings have a persuasive case. If there are clear-cut systems for assessing life learnings, then typical high school youth have as much right to life experience credit as do the constituencies usually singled out (minorities, people in special occupations, adults, and so on).

Those who argue for limiting the programs to only special groups argue that such groups have been discriminated against and were not permitted to enter college and pursue traditional forms of study. Others maintain that some individuals have had distinctive life experiences and should have this special route reserved for them. A few advocate that an age limit be established (thirty-five or forty years of age) on the grounds that people must have lived for some period in order to have had sufficient experiences from which to derive learnings that are creditable. Typically, these programs are being kept away from college youth and are being used to attract new market constituencies—individuals who would probably not attend regular college and university programs without some special recognition for what they believe they have accomplished.

Conclusion

Ultimately, decisions regarding programs for crediting life experiences will not be made on the single criterion of whether such innovations lower or update college standards. Influences such as public pressure for more varied and different programs and budgetary demands for more students will be important determinants of change.

This author's predispositions are to favor the second option in each of the fifteen issues outlined in this chapter. It may be possible to retain some vision of high quality and sound standards if these positions are thoroughly conceptualized. While it will never be possible to convince some educators that crediting prior life learnings can ever have a dimension of high quality learning, it remains incumbent on the advocates of such programs to continuously support their positions, recognize their assumptions, and reveal the strengths and weaknesses in their practices.

Although all of the issues dealt with in this chapter have been academic in nature, there are also critical economic, political, and social questions that will have great influence in shaping the movement to credit prior life learning.

More students will enroll in colleges that credit life experience. These students will be different from those presently attending; they will seek traditional forms of credit and diplomas for nontraditional kinds of accomplishments. Some of the forces and groups who will combine against the initiation of prior credit programs include: faculty who believe their standards represent high-quality, and not simply anachronistic, traditions; college administrators who believe that their institutions' images will be tarnished; community colleges, vocational schools, junior colleges, and other post-secondary institutions who perceive potential clients being lured away; graduate schools that will be forced to evaluate nontraditional students suddenly armed with bachelors degrees and seeking admission; certain employers forced to pay some of their employees more money because they have a college degree; some students in regular programs who resent awarding life experience credits which they had to struggle to "earn." Some of the forces and groups who will be active supporters for crediting students' prior life experiences include: university administrators seeking higher enrollments; faculty in need of jobs; the large number of students, faculty, and others who sincerely believe that life experiences are as potentially educative as traditional curricula; politicians who can benefit from showing they make greater use of public facilities.

Crediting prior life experiences is essentially an academic matter dealing with the issues presented in this chapter. Like most academic matters, however, the real decisions will be based on economic and political criteria. At present, it seems that the economic factors are operating in favor of opening up the university to such programs, while the political controls seem to be in the hands of those who oppose such programs. How exciting and unusual it would be if the academic issues involved were studied in depth and reported honestly. It would be interesting to see if data and systematic analyses could affect a trend of this magnitude.

Part III:
Society and Policy

Society and Policy

The policies and practices associated with education have far reaching social consequences. If the educational system mirrors, at least in part, dominant social norms of society, these norms will tend to be reenforced and perpetuated by policy makers. The perpetuation of certain belief systems through education is the focus of Part III. The transmission of these beliefs may not always be in the form of conscious policy decisions. Yet they are incorporated into the educational structure, at times in subtle and covert ways, and in time may become important influences on policy makers.

A case in point is Chapter 9 on social stereotyping in education by James Blackwell. He maintains that social stereotyping occurs throughout society and is transmitted, consciously or subconsciously, by various socializing agencies, including the school. The derogatory effects of stereotyping are perpetuated by (1) omitting minority group contributions from textbooks; (2) lack of adequate coverage of information about minority groups; (3) biased treatment of minorities as far as their unique contributions to American society; and (4) unfair assessments of minority group status in relation to dominant group positions.

For Blackwell, stereotyping is covertly transmitted through the educational system because social scientists have not adequately investigated and exposed the sources and effects of stereotyping in the larger society. Educational policy makers in turn have not sufficient data to counter stereotyping in the schools. Blackwell suggests that sound educational policy in this area should center on conducting better empirical research, interpreting research more critically, revising textbooks, and creating a better genreral understanding of how stereotypes are formed and perpetuated over time.

In Chapter 10, Terry Saario describes the efforts of the federal government to overcome another form of stereotyping based on sex discrimination. Saario describes the rationale underyling the Title IX legislation that legally forbids discrimination on the basis of sex. She argues that although the intent of the legislation was sound, there are now major problems developing in terms of substantiating cases of sex discrimination. She points out that Title IX legislation is also infringing on the traditional autonomy of such bodies as boards of education and school administrations. The central issue then becomes: Do affirmative action programs treat all persons fairly as well as equally, or do some programs discriminate against some parties? Saario concludes by outlining the important questions that must be answered by the Title IX legislation. One important area needing further clarification, for example, is how to empirically document and evaluate the cases of alleged discrimination.

In the final chapter Allan Ornstein looks at a related educational policy that is increasingly having important social consequences: the use of minority quota systems in higher education to fulfill affirmative action guidelines. The educational policy in this case is being formulated by extra-educational groups such as the federal government and its umbrella agencies, the Department of Labor and the Department of Health, Education and Welfare. Ornstein believes that the guidelines for minority group hiring in terms of faculty (in colleges and universities) are discriminatory in that they set specific quotas but say little about qualifications. One effect of this policy that he explores is "reverse discrimination." Students who would ordinarily be admitted, say to graduate or professional schools, may also be passed over for less qualified students who hold a particular minority status. In the long run, what the educational system must accomplish in terms of policy, according to Ornstein, is to strike a balance that provides opportunities for groups discriminated against in the past, while at the same time not creating new bases for discrimination against others.

Social Stereotyping and the Education Community

James E. Blackwell

In recent years the educational community has come under serious attack for research and publications that have either wittingly or unwittingly encouraged the perpetuation of unwarranted stereotypes about racial and ethnic groups. Similarly, the school and the school community have been criticized for engaging in pedagogical practices, behavioral patterns, and biased interpretations of data which also lead to stereotypical views that help to impede the learning process among minority group students. The research often suffers from faulty theoretical construction and methodological weaknesses, giving rise inevitably to erroneous interpretations of findings. And teachers too often accept these findings without careful scrutiny about their accuracy before transmitting them as truths to impressionable students.

This chapter examines the nature and scope of stereotypes and demonstrates how stereotypes are perpetuated in the educational community. In this process, suggestions will be made about how the identified pitfalls may be either avoided or overcome in future research.

Nature and Character of Stereotypes

Social scientists have been engaged in increasingly systematic research on the nature, scope, functions, and persistence of stereotypes since the 1920s, and they have been involved in trait-attribution even longer. Nevertheless, our knowledge about stereotypes is far from complete. Because of methodological weaknesses in many of the studies, there is still disagreement among social scientists on what kinds of attitudes actually constitute a stereotype, on the process involved in stereotype formation, and on how many traits are necessary for the development of a stereotype configuration. The term "stereotype" was first used by Walter Lippmann in 1922 to refer to those "little pictures," or mental images, that a person activates to "simplify and codify" his or her perceptions of a highly complex world.[1]

Since that initial interpretation of the concept was espoused, a considerable debate has followed on what constitutes a stereotype. Consequently, several definitions of the term are found in any examination of the literature on the subject. For example, some social scientists claim that "stereotypes are generalized impressions of groups acquired by individuals from a number of sources, including sometimes direct experiences with members of the stereotyped groups."[2] Others maintain that stereotypes are "the unscientific and hence unreliable generalizations that people make about other people either as persons or as groups."[3]

Still others draw distinctions between *personal* stereotypes (a single individual's assignment of a collection of traits to members of a category) and *social* stereotypes ("consensual assignments of a given population of judges").[4] And some would concentrate on ethnic groups as the major focus of stereotyped thinking and trait-assignments by referring to an ethnic stereotype as a "generalization made about an ethnic group, concerning a trait-attribution, which is considered to be unjustified by an observer. It is the observer who will decide that the generalization is or is not a stereotype, according to his criteria of justifiability."[5]

Irrespective of the interpretations of the concept employed, when stereotypes are spoken of it is done in terms of a cognitive level of orientation, that is, of beliefs about and quick ways of sizing up people. Labels such as "the fighting Irish," "the inscrutable Orientals," "the solid Swedes," "the grasping Jews," "the emotional Italians," and "the shiftless blacks" are examples.[6] Essentially, those are traits, usually negative, generalized as characteristic of an entire population. The generalizing is done in such a manner that whenever a member of a group does not fit the stereotypical image, that person is an exception to the rule. But the stereotype is neither considered invalid nor weakned in the mind of the person who has stereotyped the group.

One important early scientific study of stereotypes was conducted by Daniel Katz and Kenneth Braly on a student population at Princeton University in 1933. The students in this study were asked to identify five of a total of eighty-four traits which they thought were the "most typical" of the following ethnic groups: Americans, English, Germans, Jews, Negroes, Japanese, Italians, Chinese, Irish, and Turks. The findings followed closely to how individuals were then ranked on a social distance scale. Thus, not expectedly, the "most typical" traits of blacks were perceived in socially undesirable and negative terms. And these were far more intense than was the case with most other groups considered. For example, 84 percent of the subjects perceived blacks as "superstitious"; 75 percent thought them to be "lazy"; 38 percent referred to them as "ignorant"; 22 percent labeled them as "stupid." Other traits commonly assigned to blacks were: "happy-go-lucky," "musical," and "ostentatious." None of the remaining nine ethnic groups evoked as much uniformity of trait perceptions as did the black population.[7] It is interesting to note that the subjects in this study, many of whom had never had direct contact with black Americans except in some servile capacity, revealed attitudinal patterns and perceptions that were widely portrayed in minstrel shows, novels, jokes told by the white population, and in reference works often used in college classes.

In 1910, two decades before the Katz and Braly study at Princeton, Howard Odum, a leading sociologist of the time, had published extremely derogatory statements about the characteristics of American blacks in his widely read *Social and Mental Traits of the Negro.*[8] Also published in 1910 was a work by another prominent sociologist, Charles Ellwood, called *Sociology and Modern Social Problems.*[9] In one chapter devoted to blacks as a social problem, Ellwood assumed that blacks were characterized by a racial temperament; shiftlessness; sensuality; inferiority in adaptiveness to modern, complex societies; had lowered ambition which could best be raised by an infusion of white blood into the race; and that heredity played a significant role in the determination of those traits.

Almost a dozen years after the appearance of the Katz-Braly study, Gunnar Myrdal called attention to the pervasiveness of stereotypes among the American white population that sought to maintain the caste system as it was then. In his monumental study, *An American Dilemma,* he pointed out that "the theory of the inborn inferiority of the Negro people is . . . used as an argument for the anti-amalgamation doctrine. This doctrine, in its turn, . . . is a central position in the American system of color caste. The belief in biological inferiority is thus another basic support, in addition to the no-social equality, anti-amalgamation doctrine, of the system of segregation." Myrdal also clearly stated the role of textbooks and literature in perpetuating stereotypes in his observation that:

> . . . the Negro has met with great injustice in American literature as he has in American life. The majority of books about Negroes merely stereotype Negro character . . . all of these stereotypes are marked either by exaggeration or omission; . . . they all agree in stressing the Negro's divergence from an Anglo-Saxon norm to the flattery of the latter; . . . they all illustrate dangerous specious generalizing from a few particulars recorded by a single observer from a restricted point of view—which is itself generally dictated by a desire to perpetuate a stereotype.[10]

This theme of the codification of stereotypes and the perpetuation of them by various means was repeated again in 1949 with the publication by Maurice Davie of *Negroes in American Society.* Davie pointed to the "southern credo" regarding perceptions of white southerners about black Americans:

> The Negro is inferior and will remain so. He can never be expected to measure up to the white man's standards of character and achievement. He should be kept in his place as an inferior. This is a white man's country, and the white race must dominate. Negroes are by nature lazy and shiftless, dependent and carefree, incapable of self-discipline and forethought, inclined to criminal behavior, and sexually immoral. As an individual, he may be capable, likeable, trustworthy, and honest, but this is the exception. Finally, the whole matter is not a debatable issue.[11]

It is apparent in the observations of both Myrdal and Davie that those traits assigned or attributed to black Americans are believed to be inherent in their biological structure or genetic composition and are not a consequence of environmental conditions. Moreover, they are indiscriminately attributed to the group as a whole as group characteristics, rather than as accidents of individuality irrespective of group identification or affiliation. Further, these observations are indicative of how deeply entrenched such belief systems are in the American culture as a whole, even though the primary focus of both Myrdal and Davie was on attitudes of southern whites toward blacks. Undoubtedly such factors as persistence, intensity, tenacity, and transference of stereotypes do show some regional characteristics emanating from the peculiarities of social situations and structured relationships between groups over time. However, many are quite uniform from one part of the country to another.

Stereotypes are believed by some researchers to be persistent, while others claim that stereotypes change over time and that their variability is a function of such factors as types of groups included in the list being stereotyped and whether or not a list of traits is made available for assignment to an ethnic group.[12] In order to test the notion of persistence in stereotypes, G.M. Gilbert replicated the Katz and Braly study in 1951; Marvin Karlins and associates replicated the same study and reported their findings in 1969. Gilbert noted that, in general, those characteristics most frequently checked in the earlier Katz and Braly study were also most frequently checked in 1951. However, the uniformity in responses was considerably reduced; more adjectives were required in 1951 (at least twelve) in order to identify the five "most typical traits" assigned to blacks in 1933, for instance. Thus, Gilbert concluded that some "fading" of stereotypes had occurred in the near two decades between the two studies.[13]

Karlins and associates replicated the Katz and Braly study on 150 freshmen and sophomores at Princeton University, using the same procedures employed in the earlier study. The findings in the later study showed that over the thirty-five years since the original study at Princeton, students had come to characterize blacks in a more favorable light. Similarly, more favorable traits were assigned to the Japanese, Germans, Jews, and English than to themselves as "Americans." (The tendency to cast Europeans in general in a more favorable light because "they are like us" and to view non-Europeans less favorably, or "not like us," is so pervasive among these subjects, that it suggests a strong relationship between social distance, ethnocentrism, and stereotyping.) Although the frequency of some stereotypes declined, earlier stereotypes were replaced by new ones which, in fact, resembled earlier ones. For example, in the Katz and Braly study, Italians were considered "hot tempered." In the Karlins study, that image was replaced by a cluster of traits which included "passionate," "impulsive" and "quick tempered." Furthermore, Italians were thought to be "pleasure-loving" and "sensual."[14]

Those studies on stereotypes are important for what they reveal about persistence, replacement, and substitution of traits assigned to groups over time.

Their salience is also manifested in what the studies reveal about the kinds of attitudes that college students bring with them as a consequence of learnings in early childhood socialization and from socializing agents during the elementary and secondary school years. Further, as was pointed out in both the Gilbert and Karlins studies, college students have become reluctant to participate in stereotyping and are, in increasing numbers, raising doubts about their being forced to serve as subjects in studies of this sort. Such reluctance may reflect the negative image of formal education on tendencies to stereotype or unwillingness to generalize about specific groups of people.

Most studies focus on the negative stereotypes held by dominant group members about minority group members. Comparatively little information is available regarding the "reciprocal stereotypes" of the minority toward the dominant group. Perhaps as a consequence of the prejudice, exclusion, segregation, and discrimination directed at them, minority groups have engaged in "reactive categorization" of dominant group members as a method of restoring their pride and personal integrity. But the formation of stereotypes about the dominant group among minorities is considerably more than a defense system. It is a result of the demeaned social and economic roles that they have performed for the benefit of the dominant group, which in turn led them to perceive the dominant group in negative terms.[15]

Functions and Transmission of Stereotypes

There are two basic functions served by stereotypes. First, it is believed that stereotypes persist because they are convenient and simple ways of categorizing or labeling people. Thus, when the principle of parsimony is applied, stereotypes obviate the need for detailed descriptions when attempting to place an individual member of a stereotyped group in context. That form of convenience is, however, closely linked to prejudice against the stereotyped group. One caution is made about this observation: It may be possible to dissociate a personal stereotype from social stereotypes against the entire group. Hence, some personal stereotypes may be highly favorable in contrast to the general derogation of traits assigned to groups. But in general, stereotypes, either consciously or unwittingly, serve to perpetuate prejudice and intergroup disharmony; usually people who stereotype are also prejudiced.

The second function of stereotypes is to maintain structured patterns of dominant group superordination and minority group subordination. This justifies the social order as it is and provides arguments for adherents to stereotyped thinking against social change. If, for example, it is believed by dominant group members that the intellectual ability of a minority group is limited, this belief may be the basis for providing that group with a lower quality of education.

When it is asserted that minority group members have little mechanical aptitude, a rationalization is provided for denying them access to jobs that would help raise their standards of living. Similarly, blacks may be relegated to routinized and lower-echelon positions in the occupational structure if it is assumed, as some social scientists do, that blacks do not perform well in positions requiring abstract reasoning. Social relations between the races can be impeded by the actualization of belief systems that assign to minorities peculiarly obnoxious or hircine odors (without an appreciation of the reciprocal belief of minorities regarding dominant group members). Social proscriptions against black male-white female cohabitation and intermarriage are implicit in the stereotypes of the sexual prowess and primitive sexuality of the black male, which remain as a major component in the configuration of stereotypes about black Americans in contemporary American society. As has been pointed out, however, an increasingly larger number of individuals no longer hold such stereotypes and are inclined to treat minorities on the basis of their personal characteristics rather than on group-attributed traits.

Although we know that stereotypes are learned, it is not known precisely at what stage in a person's life that the incorporation of a belief system that includes social and personal stereotypes occurs. They are, of course, learned during various stages of the socialization process–whether early childhood, adolescent, or adult socialization and resocialization. Hence, stereotypes are transmitted, consciously or subconsciously, by various socializing agents, including family members, peer groups, reference groups, significant others, schools, teachers, and the media. Stereotypes are also perpetuated through literature, textbooks, and instructional materials used in classrooms; various forms of humor; and radio and television programs. Thus, any effort to dilute the force of ethnic and racial stereotypes must of necessity take into consideration those mechanisms used to transmit, communicate, and perpetuate them. Attacking this problem is not an easy task. However, in recent years, more and more social scientists have become concerned about the ways in which social science research is used to perpetuate negative trait-attribution about various groups of people. Consequently, they have begun to exercise greater care in the implementation of research and in interpretations of data.

The Educational Community and the Perpetuation of Stereotypes

Some of the responsibility for the persistence of derogatory and demeaning stereotypes about minority groups rests with the educational community in the United States. This situation results from at least four factors: (1) the omission of minority groups from textbooks used in classrooms; (2) inadequate coverage of information about minority groups; (3) biased treatment of minority groups in terms of their contributions to American society; and (4) unrealistic assessments of minority group status in relationship to dominant group positions in the social structure. Consequently, some researchers have argued that four conditions are required in order to satisfy what is termed "adequate coverage" of minority groups in textbooks: (1) inclusion, (2) balance, (3) comprehensiveness, and (4) realism.[16]

Frequently textbooks and other teaching materials fail to meet those criteria. For example, it has been argued that the average American text ignored the position of American blacks and that the focus of most of those which did was on the period up to the Reconstruction in American history. Consequently, many textbooks perpetuated the stereotypes of blacks as slaves, inferior, and childlike. Further, most texts examined in 1949 did not provide a serious treatment of the status of blacks in American life; nor did they provide illustrations depicting that status in a realistic manner.[17] A similar observation was made by the B'nai B'rith Anti-Defamation League in a 1960 study, which involved an examination of some forty-eight textbooks. In this study, twenty-four texts were selected for analysis on the subject of the "position of blacks in contemporary society." Of this number, thirteen failed to mention blacks in contemporary society. In many instances, whenever blacks were mentioned, their treatment was perfunctory and failed the test of comprehensiveness and balance.

Michael Kane, in his examination of forty-five texts on the subject almost a decade later, found an increasing trend toward greater inclusion of realistic information about blacks in textbooks. Less than a fourth (ten) of the books omitted reference to blacks in contemporary society, but nine of the ten were world history texts. Kane also observed that: (1) social problems texts were, as a general rule, more likely to include information about blacks; (2) only five books offered what he termed "exceptional" or "satisfactory" treatments; (3) most were inadequate in their treatment of the civil rights movement; (4) most suffered from a lack of validity by equating black power with violence; and (5) most of the descriptions of blacks lacked insight into what it means to be black in contemporary American society. Textbooks, therefore, either by their brevity, incomplete statements, inuendo, or outright statements, often unnecessarily reinforce invalid stereotypes.[18]

One consequence of the civil rights movements and its accompanying thrust of consciousness-raising among blacks have been their demands for major changes in the treatment of blacks in textbooks. Although some changes have occurred, the stereotypes remain essentially unchanged. As Kane observed, an increasing proportion of textbooks now are "ethnically balanced" and show "integrated illustrations of American life." Such illustrations depict blacks in a variety of nonstereotyped roles. For example, the diversity of occupational and family roles among blacks is evidenced in illustrations of them as physicians, scientists, nurses, lawyers, businessmen, ambassadors, congressmen, teachers, policemen, secretaries, janitors, truck drivers, and so on.[19]

Just as changes in views of blacks have occurred which depict them in a less derogatory manner, similar observations can be made about other minority groups such as Jews, Chicanos, and Japanese. Each of these groups is depicted in increasingly favorable perspectives and with less stereotyping and derogation. But in many instances, the traits that are stereotypes with respect to groups such as the Japanese and Jews are traits admired when found among members of the dominant population. White businessmen, for example, are expected to be aggressive and clever; these are admired traits in them. Yet, when the same traits are exhibited by Jews and Japanese they are perceived in unfavorable terms.

Still another problem centers around the appropriateness of the content of textbooks for some school children. Brigham and Weissnach call attention to this issue as it related to certain events that many authors and teachers blandly assume to be commonly shared experiences among school children (for example, a trip to a grandparent's farm may have no relevance for ghetto children who have never seen a farm). Brigham and Weissnach raise the question of the lack of relevance of educational materials that may not stimulate children to learn and may therefore contribute to poor academic performance.[20] Poor academic performance, triggered by inadequate educational materials and by the use of materials that have no relevance for minority children, may result in resegregation in the classroom by virtue of the assignment of students to ability groups. In this manner, certain stereotypes are reenforced and strengthened. The prejudice or insensitivity of some authors and some classroom teachers on this issue may be further illustrated by other examples. The use of such stereotypes as Little Black Sambo, and the Frito Bandito or the perpetuation of the Archie Bunker mentality or references to skin-colored (pink) bandages tend to reenforce stereotypes and suggest the proverbial germ of truth in their derogation of minority group members.

Insensitivity to language differences and the various usages of the same language also helps to entrench negative trait-attribution and perceptions of minority group children. It is only in recent years that many school systems have recognized the value of bilingual education for some minority groups. Similarly, only recently have educators become sensitive to the fact that a disregard for language barriers has heightened perceptions of the uneducability of some children. Literally thousands of Spanish-speaking children have been classified as retarded because of their performance on tests administered in English. As many as 22,000 Spanish-speaking children in California previously classified as "unfit for normal schooling," were retested under a court order following a class-action suit brought by Rural League assistant attorneys in California.[21]

Stereotypes about the inability of minority group children and children from low-income families to read may also result from language problems that stem from differences in semantic development and in interpretations of the English language. For example, Doris Entwisle and Ellen Greenberger reported that:

> Educational deficits and reading problems in disadvantaged children may be more a function of semantic [under] development than has been hitherto supposed . . . [I]n spite of an early spurt in syntatic development, . . . first-grade black inner-city children give responses that are less mature in terms of semantic content than those of white children. . . . The fact that semantic structures are different for blacks and whites at the time of school entrance may be a great hinderance to learning reading, for the cues in primers and basal readers may be inappropriate.[22]

The authors also claim that the differences observed are associated with IQ and with social class. However, it should be understood that what may be defined as "semantic underdevelopment" is in itself a dysfunction between subcultural or class linked language patterns or both and the linguistic expectations of the classroom situation. It is possible that black children in the inner city have an excellent command of language requirements which enable them to function effectively in that social situation. However, because of their lack of facility with the language of various performance and achievement tests, they may be classified as linguistically underdeveloped and retarded. Richard Lederer and Robert Hall examine this issue:

> Assuming that all our language patterns are British in derivation, linguists and English teachers have regarded Afro-American variations as ignorant mis-usages of standard English, ignoring the African background of the Afro-American English ("cat," for example, is a West African word for "person") and the obvious indications that it is a subtle and precise language, following its own rules. In addition, study after study shows that Afro-American language is in no way cognitively deficient in comparison with other dialects.[23]

One implication of such assumptions is that people who do not speak precisely within the normative boundaries established by the dominant group are, by definition, ignorant. This is especially the case when their subcultural language is ranked lower than the language of work, government, and the society at large. The more often this situation is evident, the more pervasive the stereotype about the out-group.

Although a societal expectation is that all school children should develop those language skills that are necessary for functioning in the society as a whole, in contrast to functioning in a subcultural milieu, tests of linguistic ability should take into consideration a person's capacity to communicate what is known about the world that is closest to his everyday life as well as to the world outside. Moreover, it seems incumbent upon the teachers in inner-city schools to do a more effective job of working with students who are recognized as semantically underdeveloped. Furthermore, according to Daniel Levine, improving skills and reading readiness may require "smaller classes, more suitable curricular materials and instructional methods . . . pre-kindergarten classes emphasizing the development of cognitive skills," and personalized attention in order to compensate for educational deficits among inner-city children and children from low-income families.[24]

Again, social science researchers and classroom teachers can play a most effective role in either diluting or eliminating the potency of stereotypes. Several researchers have pointed out, for instance, that minority group children bring to school distinctive experiences that have a special salience for their subculture. Aside from language differences, they may include such things as divergent orientations toward achievement, life styles, values, and different stereotypes about dominant group people. Thus, their behavior and their performance on achievement tests, intelligence tests, and aptitude tests may be particularly affected by preconditioned cultural attitudes. Yet, misunderstandings occur as a result of both teachers and researchers failing to appreciate these differences in their interpretations of performance and behavior.[25] That is precisely why the current polemics surrounding the validity of IQ tests, performance tests, and measures of positive or negative self-concepts among minority group children persists. Therein lies an important explanation for the persistence of related stereotypes in the educational community.

The failure of researchers to move forward in the breaking of stereotypes has been amply documented in separate essays by Andrew Billingsley. The focus of Billingsley's views is primarily on misconceptions about the black family. He maintains that "American social scientists . . . reflect all the prejudice, ignorance, and arrogance which seems to be endemic to Americans of European descent." He also argues that social scientists, because of their communication skills, contribute more to misunderstandings about black family life than do ordinary citizens. He supports his position by analyses of various texts and references on family structure and life authored by American social scientists. Billingsley shows that some of the leading texts on the family do not meet the four criteria for adequate treatment previously discussed (inclusion, balance, comprehensiveness, and realism). For example, Bell and Vogel's *A Modern Introduction to the Family* (1968) includes only one article on black families from a total of fifty-two in the anthology. Parsons and Bales, in *Family, Socialization and Interaction Process* (1960), do not mention the concept "Negro" in the subject index. Billingsley points out that in *Urban Society* (1964), a 600-page text by Gist and Fava, one page is devoted to the Puerto Rican families in New York, not even a full page is given to African families, and not one single line is given to black families in urban America. He demonstrates the problem of omission again in Kephart's *The Family, Society, and the Individual* (1966), which does not devote even one of its twenty-three chapters to black family life. In Marvin Sussman's *Sourcebook in Marriage and Family* (1959), one of its sixty-two articles is devoted to marriage between blacks and whites; no chapter deals with black couples.[26]

The notion of a "tangle of pathology" within black families is also perpetuated by social science literature. This tendency has been observed in recent years in the treatment given to black families by the sociologist Daniel Moynihan in *The Negro Family: The Case For National Action* (1965). This report has been severely criticized for inaccurate analysis of the data presented, bias in the analysis of findings, and unwarranted assertions that the black family existed in a tangle of pathology. Several writers have argued against and discredited Moynihan's interpretations and assumptions. Of special concern are his suggestions that the black family is largely matriarchal and his negative assertions regarding high rates of illegitimacy. Even at the time of the Moynihan report more than two-thirds of all black families were headed by males or contained two parents. That a majority of black families were male-headed would not suggest disorganization using family head as the indicator of stability in the society as a whole.[27] Hence, it appears that if black families are not altogether ignored in the major texts on family life authored by white social scientists, the tendency is to focus primary attention on the "pathological conditions" of the underclass black families as if they were the norm rather than the exception. Rarely do such authors describe the strengths of black families. Neither is adequate attention devoted to those cohesive forces within the majority of black families which bind them together as stable social units. This glaring omission undoubtedly has led black scholars to fill this void, as did Robert Hill in *Strengths of Black Families.*[28]

Billingsley cites four reasons to account for this poor treatment of the black family: (1) the family as a social institution has not been given adequate treatment by social scientists, irrespective of racial considerations; (2) dominance of whites in the social sciences who have not been as concerned about the institutional life of black people as they have about whites; (3) failure to recognize the research of black scholars or black students of black family life; and (4) the nature of the discipline that relies so heavily, in its methodology, upon statistical techniques and theoretical speculations.[29] As a consequence, stereotypes are continually transmitted, and myths or misconceptions are perpetuated in such a manner as to have negative impact on both the content of what is learned about black families and the effectuation of policies that will help black families to retain their strengths and positive attributes.

Public opinion is certainly influenced by reports from social scientists that fatherless homes cause boys to become delinquents and by research that provides incomplete information on illegitimacy rates and numbers of low-income minorities on public assistance. Far too many of the studies oversimplify associations between fatherlessness and male delinquency in much the same way that they oversimplify associations between what is viewed as a matriarchal structure and "demasculinization" among boys reared in homes without a father. Herzog points out that the assumptions upon which such associations are based are often dubious and result from studies flawed by serious methodological weaknesses.[30]

And it is not sufficient to say that blacks are disproportionately represented in public assistance or welfare rolls for this leaves the impression that the majority of people on welfare or who receive aid to families with dependent children are black. This is completely erroneous. Although it is true that blacks are overrepresented among welfare recipients in terms of their population ratios, the overwhelming majority of welfare recipients are white. In addition, the middle- and upper-class white population receives other forms of welfare in far greater proportions than is the case for blacks and other minorities. Specifically, the "white middle class receives a far greater share of FHA loans than do blacks" and even more assistance in the form of federal subsidization of bankrupt corporations in the defense industry in contrast to the paltry sums of money granted by the federal government for the capitalization of minority business enterprises.[31]

Regarding the misconceptions about differential rates of illegitimacy between blacks and whites, Herzog contends that

> . . . these stereotypes are perpetuated by the fact that critics often fail to take into account other variables such as socioeconomic status, the gathering of statistics, differences in the readiness to marry due to pregnancy, and the availability of abortions. If these factors were considered, the alleged high illegitimacy rates of blacks would be substantially reduced.[32]

Conclusion

This chapter has examined the nature and scope of stereotypes and demonstrated how they are both transmitted and perpetuated in the educational community. It has also attempted to show that persistent stereotypes are utilized to maintain the dominance of one group over others and to reinforce social distance, ethnocentrism, and isolation between groups within the same society. Although it is not known precisely when a person learns stereotypes, it is certain that, as learned behavior, stereotypes are transmitted and perpetuated through the various agents responsible for childhood and adult socialization. Just as the family, peers, and members of the educational community are significant others in this process, textbooks and other learning aides are of importance in acquiring and reinforcing stereotypes.

It might be argued that social scientists and educators in general can help to eliminate the use of stereotypes in the educational community by: (1) conducting research that is based upon sound theoretical concepts and well-planned methodologies; (2) becoming more precise and accurate but less biased in their interpretations of research findings; (3) including more comprehensive information about minority group life and contributions in textbooks, particularly in the social sciences; (4) presenting a fairer and more balanced treatment of minority groups in instructional materials; and (5) by augmenting the knowledge about stereotypes by creating a better understanding of the process of their formation and of the factors that affect their intensity, direction, and uniformity over time.

Notes

1. See John Brigham and Theodore Weissnach, eds., *Racial Attitudes in America* (New York: Harper & Row, 1972).
2. Marvin Karlins, Thomas Coffman, and Gary Walters, "On the Fading of Social Stereotypes: Studies in Three Generations of College Students," *Journal of Personality and Social Psychology* 13 (1969): 4.
3. Emory S. Bogardus, "Stereotypes versus Sociotypes," *Sociology and Social Research* 34 (1950): 287.
4. See Karlins, Coffman, and Walters, "Three Generations of College Students"; and Paul F. Secord and Carl W. Backman, *Social Psychology* (New York: McGraw-Hill, 1964), p. 3.
5. John C. Brigham, "Ethnic Stereotypes," *Psychological Bulletin* 76 (1971): 31.
6. James Vander Zanden, *American Minority Relations* (New York: Ronald Press, 1972).
7. Daniel Katz and Kenneth W. Braly, "Racial Stereotypes of 100 College Students," *Journal of Abnormal Psychology* 28 (1933): 280-290.
8. Howard W. Odum, *Social and Mental Traits of the Negro* (New York: Columbia University, 1910).
9. Charles A. Ellwood, *Sociology and Modern Social Problems* (New York: American Book Company, 1910).
10. Gunnar Myrdal, *An American Dilemma* (New York: Harper & Row, 1944), pp. 102 and 1196.
11. Maurice R. Davie, *Negroes in American Society* (New York: McGraw-Hill, 1949), pp. 364-365.
12. Brigham and Weissnach, *Racial Attitudes in America.*
13. G.M. Gilbert, "Stereotype Persistence and Change among College Students," *Journal of Abnormal and Social Psychology* 46 (1951): 245-254.
14. Karlins, Coffman, and Walters, "Three Generations of College Students."
15. For a discussion of reciprocal stereotypes, see Judith R. Kramer, *The American Minority Community* (New York: Crowell, 1970); and Geneva Fay and Roger D. Abrahams, "Does the Pot Melt, Boil, or Brew: Black Children and White Assessment Procedures," *Journal of School Psychology* 11 (1973): 330-340.
16. Michael Kane, *Minorities in Textbooks* (New York: B'nai B'rith Anti-Defamation League, 1970).

17. Ibid.

18. Ibid.

19. Ibid.

20. Brigham and Weissnach, *Racial Attitudes in America.*

21. Ibid.

22. Doris R. Entwisle and Ellen Greenberger, "Racial Differences in the Language of Grade School Children," *Sociology of Education* 42 (1969): 238-250.

23. Richard Lederer and Robert L. Hall, "Language and the Minority Student," *Independent School Bulletin* 33 (1974): 35-37.

24. Daniel U. Levine, "Stratification, Segregation, and Children in the Inner-City School," *School and Society* 98 (1970): 88.

25. See Nathan Glazer, "Ethnic Groups and Education: Towards the Tolerance of Difference," *Journal of Negro Education* 38 (1969): 187-195; and Benjamin J. Hodgkins and Robert G. Stakenas, "A Study of Self-Concepts of Negro and White Youth in Segregated Environments," *Journal of Negro Education* 38 (1969): 370-377.

26. Andrew Billingsley, "Black Families and White Social Science," *Journal of Social Issues* 26 (1970): 127-142.

27. See ibid.; and Elizabeth Herzog, "Social Stereotypes and Social Research," *Journal of Social Issues* 26 (1970): 109-125; James E. Blackwell, *The Black Community: Diversity and Unity* (New York: Dodd, Mead, 1975); and Robert Hill, *The Strengths of Black Families* (New York: Emerson Hall, 1972), for a more detailed discussion of these points.

28. Ibid.

29. Billingsley, "Black Families and White Social Science."

30. Herzog, "Social Stereotypes and Social Research."

31. Blackwell, *Black Community.*

32. Herzog, "Social Stereotypes and Social Research."

10 Title IX: Now What?

Terry N. Saario

In June 1975 Casper Weinberger, then secretary of the Department of Health, Education and Welfare, announced the issuance of regulations for the administration and enforcement of Title IX of the 1972 Education Amendments.[a] On 21 July 1975, with the approval of Congress, Title IX became law.[b] That date should prove, over time, to be an historic landmark in the history of American education. After three years in which its detractors and supporters maneuvered for control of its definition, Title IX became the law of the land and, as such, was the broadest prescription against sex discrimination in education to have emerged from Congress. Specifically, Title IX states: "No person in the United States shall, on the basis of sex, be excluded from participation in, be denied the benefits of, or be subjected to discrimination under any education program or activity receiving federal financial assistance . . ."[1] Its sponsors viewed the law as a way to close a statutory loophole in Title VI of the Civil Rights Act of 1964. Its detractors viewed Title IX as additional evidence of federal encroachment upon the constitutional purview and domain of the states. These differences have not been resolved and are likely to become even more exacerbated as efforts are made to bring a variety of educational institutions and agencies into full compliance with the law. What these efforts are likely to be and which political, social, and economic constraints are likely to affect them is the focus of this chapter.

[a]This chapter will be limited to an analysis of Title IX and its impact upon public elementary and secondary schools in the United States. A thorough and comprehensive analysis of the position of women in higher education can be found in *Opportunities for Women in Higher Education: A Report of the Carnegie Commission on Higher Education* (New York: McGraw-Hill, 1973).

[b]Title IX frequently serves as a shorthand for a battery of federal and state laws and regulations which prohibit discrimination on the basis of sex. In addition to Title IX, most important among these are: Title VII of the Civil Rights Act of 1964 as amended by the Equal Employment Opportunity Act of 1972; the Equal Pay Act of 1963 as amended by the Education Amendments of 1972; and Part II of Executive Order 11246 as amended by Executive Order 11375, state equal rights amendments, and state labor and fair employment practices statutes. While these statutes cover employment, education, credit, social security, and other equally important facets of life, Title IX is the only legislative enactment specifically prohibiting discrimination in elementary and secondary schools, colleges, and universities. (See Education Commission of the States, *A Digest of Federal Laws: Equal Rights for Women in Education*, report no. 61 (Washington, D.C.: U.S. Government Printing Office, 1975).

Background

Title IX has had an unusual history in a number of ways. It took three years for the Department of Health, Education and Welfare to issue its regulations; those regulations in draft form elicited roughly 10,000 public comments. In a unique and unprecedented move, Congress allowed a forty-five-day period to review the administration's final regulations before they became law.

What is Title IX? Why did it receive such a highly politicized and emotionally charged reaction? Title IX is a sweeping pronouncement, affecting all levels of educational practice.[2] While its major impact will be felt at the local school district level, Title IX's regulations apply equally to state departments of education personnel, federal bureaucratic personnel, state boards of education, school boards, unions indirectly, and other groups tangentially related to education. Its mandate is broad. It prohibits discrimination on the basis of sex against most adults employed in educational settings and most students who spend a significant portion of their lives in these settings. Men and women are to receive the same benefits and opportunities for job advancement; boys and girls are to receive the same instruction and treatment without regard to their gender. Only a few domains fall outside its purview. Curriculum materials, for example, have been excluded from Title IX's coverage because of a legal judgment that their inclusion would violate the constitutional guarantee of freedom of speech under the First Amendment. The membership policies of the Girl and Boy Scouts, the YMCA and YWCA, and other single sex "youth service organizations" are also exempt, albeit for different reasons.[3]

Many of the philosophical dilemmas inherent in the American system of government and in its democratic ideals are laid bare by Title IX. It is customary in America to assume a direct linkage between the best interests of society and the best interest of the individual. Unfortunately, as the last fifteen years have demonstrated, that linkage is easily shattered when the economic, political, or social interests of a particular group are directly threatened by the sometimes contradictory causes of equity and equality. Proponents of Title IX assumed a direct relationship between the best interests of society and the individual. They assumed that underutilization of approximately half of the nation's populace was not only a loss to those individuals but a significant loss to society as well. It was a cumulative loss, one that was magnified with each generation. One way to rectify this imbalance was through the schools. Schools traditionally had been one system for launching people into the world of economic gain and productive livelihood. If schools could respond to their students, without prejudice and without stereotype, perhaps the next generation would be afforded greater opportunities to determine the fibre of their lives.

Thus, Title IX was designed to right the wrongs of an educational system that, consciously or unconsciously, with or without malice, had for decades patently discriminated against women and girls. Yet this legislative enactment did not exist in a vacuum. It is not without significance that Title IX became law in 1975. The condition of education in 1975 differed markedly from that of the early 1970s, when perceptive observers of the educational enterprise noted that public school enrollments were dropping and the fiscal base for education at the federal, state, and local levels was no longer expanding. These observations led many to comment upon the implications these "no growth" indicators would have for education. But not even the most pessimistic adequately projected the state of education in 1975.

Title IX became law as the cost of education continued to rise, as taxpayers resisted increases in local taxes; as the debate over equity in financing of public schools matured into a serious examination of state and local tax policy; as enrollments continued to drop from the highs of the 1960s; and as tensions heightened between citizen groups, unions, legislators, school boards, and local administrators over control of the school and its resources. It became law as questions were raised about the utility of educational credentials; the value of education to work; and the adequacy of the educational system for the multiplicity of groups it serves. It became law as more foment and discord confronted concerned educators than had existed in decades. What a different world Title IX would have faced if it had been part of the Civil Rights Act of 1964.

While some would argue that the Title IX language in the Education Amendments of 1972 could be construed as merely a prohibition against sexually discriminatory practices in educational agencies, the implementing regulations issued in the summer of 1975 specifically require affirmative steps to be taken to remove discriminatory practices from educational settings. The distinction between a *prohibition* and *required affirmative action* is important. A requirement to cease or abandon discriminatory or exclusionary practices is not the same as a charge to take positive and overt action to alter institutional behavior and rectify previous wrongs. As an example, the general provisions of Title IX require institutional self-evaluations within one year of the date of the regulation. These evaluations are supposed to establish a baseline of current student admissions practices, treatment of students, and academic or nonacademic personnel employment policies. Practices or policies found in violation of Title IX are to be modified, and appropriate steps are to be taken to eliminate their effects. Thereafter each institution receiving federal funds is required to designate one individual to coordinate compliance efforts and to adopt grievance procedures for the resolution of student and employee complaints. If, after these mechanisms are established, a case of sex discrimination is found by the Department of Health, Education and Welfare Office of Civil Rights, an institution may then be required to take specific remedial action to overcome the effect of the discrimination. In the absence of such a finding, an institution may voluntarily take affirmative steps to overcome the effects of restricted participation by members of one gender.

Clearly, what constitutes a workable definition of affirmative action, or remedial action, or other equally ambiguous phrases used to connote the removal of discriminatory practices from educational settings, has not been resolved. Because of such ambiguity and because of enormous differences in value orientations toward the issue of discrimination, the process of defining reasonable goals for the schools will be fraught with battles that can be mustered in educational politics. What issues, then, are most likely to prompt these battles? They revolve around two distinct clientele: the adults most affected by employment considerations, and the students whose lives and aspirations are shaped by pedagogical and administrative practices in schools.

Adults: Employment Issues

Title IX incorporates many of the provisions of Title VII of the 1964 Civil Rights Act and the Equal Pay Act of 1963 and, as such, provides extensive antidiscrimination rules in the area of employment. It applies broadly to recruitment; advertising for employment; hiring; upgrading of positions; promotion; contracting and awarding of tenure; demotion; transfer; layoff; rehiring; pay rates; job assignments and seniority; the terms of collective bargaining agreements; pregnancy leaves and leaves for either males or females who must care for children; fringe benefits; selection and financial support for training; employer-sponsored activities; and any other term, condition, or privilege of employment.

The intent of the legislation is clear. Women should be afforded all the opportunities for job access and promotion that white males have received for generations. As has been frequently noted, even though education has traditionally been a "women's field" (67 percent of all public school teachers are women), more men than women are selected for administrative positions.[4] In fact, the last bastion of female administrators–elementary school principalship–is gradually being dominated by males. As the National Education Association (NEA), the National Association of Elementary School Principals (NAESP), and other organizations have shown, there has been a 2 percent per year decline among female administrators for the last several years.[5] The reasons most cited for this gradual disappearance will only become more exaggerated during the next few years. Reduction and consolidation of districts frequently requires the elimination of a number of administrative positions. Decreasing enrollments may in some instances lead to the closing of underutilized schools and the subsequent loss of administrative positions. And the professionalization of administration has frequently granted administrative positions higher status and rewards in the education community, consequently attracting a large male constituency.[6] As the premium on jobs increases with job scarcity, it could be predicted that lateral or upward mobility in administrative positions would probably decrease.

Thus, within this model, the administrative pool would become largely synonymous with a reduced rank of aging white, male administrators. Superimpose upon this statistic the Title IX provision that states school districts may not "maintain separate lines of progression, seniority lists, career ladders, or tenure systems based on sex"; an obvious collision course appears.

One ironic aspect of the long struggle in support of Title IX is that compliance decisions will most frequently be in the hands of white, male administrators. Beyond the question of protective self-interest lies a series of questions which might be answered differently if women were in greater abundance at the upper levels of the educational hierarchy. Purposeful affirmative action–the upgrading and training of women for both teaching and administrative positions, establishing internships for women interested in administrative positions, and reducing pay differentials, for example–would require a substantial reallocation of finite resources. In a budget in which roughly 80 percent of the total is already earmarked for salaries, the weighing of affirmative action alternatives becomes acute. Nevertheless, decisions brought after careful examination of contingencies could differ markedly according to how affirmative action goals were reached in a particular value system.

Discrimination is perhaps more rife among noncredentialed or noncertified school personnel. Strict adherence to the use of credentials, frequently established by state statute, assures a chasm between teachers and administrators, on the one hand, and teachers' assistants, cafeteria workers, librarians, and custodians on the other. With upward mobility into professional positions blocked by credential requirements, equal pay for equal work is an even more important consideration to this sector of the education labor market. There are at least two distinct types of employees affected by antidiscrimination legislation: the professional, or credentialed, and the blue collar, or clerical. Demands for access and equity in the two sectors are likely to be different in their details. Their effects, in terms of fears engendered and political ramifications, should be quite alike. Employee organizations and unions have a clear obligation to protect the interests of their female members, especially when they represent 60 to 70 percent of the membership in an organization controlled by white males. Yet, with increasing costs in the educational enterprise and a growing excess of employees, a union may be confronted with contradictory demands for representation on the part of its senior male members and those who acquired positions as a result of recently adopted affirmative action policies. There have already been cases of school boards attempting to protect gains made under affirmative action programs by exempting minority and female employees from layoffs. In several cases, employee organizations "have instituted legal action to block preferential retention of persons hired under affirmative action programs. In other instances, the same organizations have gone to court to block adoption of affirmative action programs."[7] The bargaining table is another area in which potential conflict may arise. Contracts that provide for discrimination in fringe benefits are illegal, as would be contracts that provide for unequal pension benefits for female employees or exclude maternity coverage from health plans.

All these concerns are on the input, or access, aside of the equation, where discrimination is fairly easy to document. If there was concern for example, with the question of whether women have had equal access to administrative positions in the past, it would be a simple matter to compute a ratio of the number of women who hold administrative credentials to the number who hold such positions and compare this statistic to similar ratios for men. Such comparisons would demonstrate whether men and women have been eased up the administrative ladder with the same proportionality or frequency. But such comparisons beg what some would argue is a more important question. Quantity presumably is not equivalent to quality, and qualitative differentials are more difficult to assess. Few good measures of administrative ability are available in the world of educational measurement. What is acceptable evidence of administrative skill? Is the principal or superintendent who has been able to retain his or her position longer than five years a successful administrator, or is longevity evidence of someone who is unwilling to take risks and of mediocre leadership? Meaningful quantification of such outputs will be a long time coming in educational research.

What of the cumulative effects of discrimination? Should a definition of remedial action take note of the informal mechanisms for promotion and leadership in education and the implicit ways in which individuals over time have been groomed for policy making positions? What steps would have to be taken to counteract the effects of being removed from years of such socialization? What costs is society willing to incur in order to achieve a goal of full participation? Not only are the provisions of Title IX ambiguous and difficult to operationalize, but they also represent a direct challenge to the local authority and autonomy of school boards and administrators. School districts are under a clear obligation, constitutional and statutory, to repair the effects of previous discrimination. Assuming good will and voluntary compliance with the law, what would constitute affirmative action? What statistical indicators of progress in eliminating discrimination would suffice under Title IX? What limits, statistically and over time, should be placed around these indicators? Should the goals and expectations acknowledge the social and economic reality in which they would be applied? Some states had adopted their own affirmative action policies prior to the issuance of Title IX. What has their experience been? Should stress be placed upon inputs or upon outputs? What would constitute sufficient, prima facie evidence of good will in a courtroom?

Those are only a few of the questions being asked by those who voluntarily want to comply with the regulations. What of those who wish to ignore Title IX's provisions or deliberately subvert the intent of the law? "If HEW determines that a recipient has failed to comply with statutes, and if the noncompliance cannot be corrected by informal means, compliance may be affected by the suspension or termination of . . . federal financial assistance."[8] Unfortunately, enforcement of such negative sanctions is always problematical at best. HEW is generally loathe to terminate funds. Moreover, with the issuance of Title IX, HEW also released a proposed consolidated procedural regulation which would govern the enforcement not only of Title IX but also of Title VI of the Civil Rights Act of 1964 and other civil rights laws under its jurisdiction. This regulation would shift the burden of HEW's responsibilities to the documentation of *systemic* discrimination in educational institutions, as opposed to investigating *individual* complaints of discrimination. If this regulation is adopted, the Department of Health, Education and Welfare would, by shifting the weight of its responsibilities, place a heavy burden upon those who are being discriminated against. The burden of proof would remain with the victims.

Students: Educational Issues

Sex discrimination affecting students takes many forms, some more manifest than others. Large numbers of textbooks and instructional materials presently in use in schools are clearly sex stereotyped and biased. Vocational education programs are frequently sex segregated. Few secondary schools provide girls with equal access to physical education and competitive sports programs. Instructional and counseling services provided for students generally support and reinforce stereotyped attitudes and behaviors about appropriate roles for males and females in society. Title IX's broad prescriptions now make many of these practices, not only morally and ethically wrong, but also illegal: "No person shall, on the basis of sex, be excluded from participation in, be denied the benefits of, or be subjected to discrimination under any academic, extracurricular, research, occupational training or any other education program or activity operated by a recipient of federal funds." While on the surface this regulation would appear to be quite easy to implement, its long-term impact should substantially alter most educational programs as they are known today. For example, assuming a school district of moderate size and enrollment, how would its school board and administrators answer the following questions?

1. In your elementary and secondary schools, are there courses or extracurricular activities that are restricted to students of only one gender?
2. Are athletic programs for male and female students comparable?
3. Are students selected on a differential basis for participation in school-related activities?
4. Do students have equal access to job placement services?
5. Are different aptitude and vocational interest tests given to male and female students?
6. Are the same counseling procedures used with male and female students?[9]

A candid answer to most of those questions would reveal gross discriminatory practices. Unfortunately such answers are not peculiar to a few school districts but rather accurately describe the situation in most of the 16,000 public school districts in America today.

Ambiguities again abound. If a school does not prohibit girls from enrolling in automobile mechanics classes but none do, has the school pursued discriminatory practices? If boys and girls enroll in equal numbers in a vocational education class, and boys are the majority of those who seek employment in that area, has the school discriminated against its female students? If a school board, facing a budget crisis, elects to discontinue a music program in which male and female enrollments are roughly equal instead of an interscholastic sports program in which males are greatest in evidence, has it discriminated against its female students? More importantly, is the school subject to a complaint of systemic discrimination? Few of these questions can be answered with ease or precedent.

Pursuit of an all-encompassing definition of discrimination as it appears in elementary and secondary schools may be diversionary and enervating. In some areas—athletics and vocational education being the two most blatant—statistics tell all that needs to be told with great drama. For example, during fiscal year 1972, more than $1.7 billion in federal, state, and local funds were expended on high school vocational education programs. More than 7 million students, of whom 66 percent were female, enrolled in these programs. Roughly 75 percent of the women were clustered in either consumer-homemaking or office skills vocational courses, while 58 percent of the males obtained training in technical, industrial, or agricultural skills.[10]

Segregation does not stop with tracking males and females into different courses. The vocational courses in which females are the majority have higher teacher-student ratios than do the technical programs in which males are the majority. Expenditures on vocational programs follow the same pattern. Over 60 percent of the total expenditures for vocational education at the high school level are earmarked for technical and industrial courses. In other words, 40 percent of the resources available for high school vocational programs are distributed to courses in which 66 percent of the students are enrolled.[11]

Simple descriptive statistics usually establish prima facie evidence of discrimination in vocational education courses. Admittedly, this skirts the question of the real utility of such courses—the question of whether, in any qualitative sense, vocational education leads to gainful employment over a lifetime of work. Descriptive statistics tell the same story in most high school sports programs. The proportion of a school's budget allocated to male interscholastic and intramural athletic programs always outstrips that allocated to women's sports programs. The discrimination is glaring; the utility of the activity in terms of a lifetime of access and fulfillment is less clear.

There are thornier questions that ought to be addressed at some point by both the supporters and antagonists of antidiscriminatory legislation. Just as we do not know what constitutes a good administrator, other than on an intuitive basis, we know embarassingly little about how sexual identities are formed and even less about the saliency or significance of gender identity in the formation and maturation of a healthy individual. Even the most authorative source on the development of sex differences available today, *The Psychology of Sex Differences*, acknowledges looming voids in our knowledge of what makes boys and girls, men and women different.[12]

Implementation of Title IX

Notwithstanding the definitional ambiguity surrounding Title IX, the need for acceptable standards or goals that can withstand politics and law, oversimplified notions about the etiology of sex differences, an inadequate research base, and serious unknowns about the consequences of action, Title IX *is* law. It is incumbent upon the educational system to move with dispatch into full compliance with the law. But why is enforcement potentially such a ticklish problem? Unlike major social reforms that the populace rallies around, the area of women's rights is in general poorly understood. As a result, it has not received the full endorsement of society. All of us have been socialized, to varying degrees, into the society in which we live. As anthropologists point out, being able to step outside one's world and look inward with the same clarity of vision that one might bring to an examination of another culture is difficult. Because our rituals, roles, and accepted patterns of behavior—the behavioral rules of our society—are basically comfortable, many of us fail to note the potent and robust forms of discrimination that by ritual and verse are inherent in many of the roles. More importantly, we frequently fail to understand how restrictive and, in the long run, how detrimental these patterns can be.

As is true in all social movements, the vanguard of the women's rights movement is far ahead of its constituency in understanding the issues. The thrust for full compliance with the law comes from these quarters. Their means range from gentle political persuasion at the local school board level to that most powerful of last resorts, litigation. A variety of efforts, for example, are presently underway to compel the federal government to address various aspects of the overall problem of sex discrimination in education. Private attorneys and public interest legal entities, such as the NOW Legal Defense and Education Fund and the Women's Rights Project of the Center for Law and Social Policy, are actively engaged in efforts to eliminate blatant forms of discrimination through suits against HEW for failure to implement the law.[13] Other groups are pressuring for direct federal assistance for measures designed to acquaint girls with a range of career training opportunities, for programs to retrain guidance counselors and other school personnel, for the elimination of aptitude tests and interest inventories that reflect sexist biases,[14] and for other mechanism to remove discriminatory practices from school-based vocational courses.

Advocates are working with similar verve and dedication at the state and local levels of education. Community-based groups worried about sexually discriminatory practices in their schools are now so numerous that it would be impossible to list them all. State commissions on the status of women have, with varying degrees of sophistication, tackled the problem of discriminatory language and sanctioned practices in state statutes. Others are informing state governments of their responsibilities under Title IX and other antidiscrimination legislation at the state level.

While the dedication and talent brought to these efforts is impressive, success in removing sexually discriminatory practices from public education will undoubtedly be mixed over the next decade, if for no other reason than an inadequate level of public understanding of the issues. As has been noted elsewhere, "legislatures and courts at all levels, reflecting views held in many parts of American society, perceive sex discrimination as less onerous or less invidious than discrimination based on race, color, or national origin."[15] A direct analogy can be drawn between the lack of public understanding of the issues and where the school finance field was in the late 1960s. At that time the field of school finance was emerging from a long period of stability, partially in response to the demands of poor and minority groups for quality education, and partially because "constitutional questions and broadened political parameters redefined traditional school finance politics." The next five years or so were full of stumbling starts and stops, with avenues for reform blocked by judicial decisions in some states and great advances promulgated by courts and legislatures in others. At the same time, a new generation of young scholars were attracted to the school finance field–lawyers, economists, political scientists, and public policy scholars.[16] With this influx of new and creative talent, different questions were asked about equity and school performance, new measures of these phenomena were defined, and a heightened public awareness of the area of school finance was achieved.

Conclusion

In some ways the area of affirmative action in public education is in an even more elementary state than was the field of school finance in the late 1960s. Public policy analysts and serious scholars have only begun to focus their attention on the area. Thorny questions about when and how to intervene in the development of a child's sexual identity need to be examined, and rigorous analyses of the costs of affirmative action in education under the fiscal constraints of the late 1970s must be performed. Coalitions with other excluded groups and with those in policy making positions need to be formed, and a massive public information campaign needs to be launched.

Ultimately, real equality between men and women and boys and girls will be achieved when the public and concerned mothers and fathers understand the ways in which schools are placing a dampener on their children's lives. Or, as the commissioner of education in the state of New York recently noted, "Equality is not when a female Einstein gets promoted to Assistant Professor; Equality is when a female schlemiel moves ahead as fast as a male schlemiel."[17]

Notes

1. Public Law No. 93-568, 88 Stat. 1855.

2. A concise overview of the Title IX regulations can be obtained in Resource Center on Sex Roles in Education, *Research Action Notes* (Washington, D.C.: National Foundation for the Improvement of Education, 1975).

3. The "Bayh amendment" to Title IX.

4. Catherine D. Lyon and Terry N. Saario, "Women in Public Education: Sexual Discrimination in Promotions," *Phi Delta Kappan* 10 (1973): 120-123.

5. John McLure and Gail McLure, "The Case of the Vanishing Woman: Implications for the Preparation of Women in Educational Administration," *UCEA Review* (September 1974): 6-9.

6. These trends may reverse slightly if June Sklar and Beth Berkow's population forecasts hold. *Science* (29 August 1975): 693-700.

7. Suzanne Martinez, "Affirmative Action and Public Education: Some Preliminary Issues and Questions," *Youth Law Center* (September 1975): 1-18.

8. Resource Center, *Research Action Notes*, p. 8.

9. Education Commission of the States, "Handbook on Title IX," mimeographed (Washington, D.C., 1975).

10. Shirley McCune, "Vocational Education: A Dual System," *Inequality in Education* 16 (1974): 28-34.

11. Marilyn Steele, "Women in Vocational Education" (Project Baseline, Northern Arizona University, 1974).

12. Eleanor E. Maccoby and Carol N. Jacklin, *The Psychology of Sex Differences* (Stanford, Calif.: Stanford University Press, 1974).

13. *Women's Equity Action League et al. vs. Mathews*, filed 27 November 1974, Civil Action No. 74-1720 (D.D.C.).

14. The two best sources currently available on bias in educational testing and career interest inventories are Carol K. Tittle, *Women and Educational Testing* (Princeton, N.J.: Educational Testing Service, 1974); and Esther E. Diamond, ed., *Issues of Sex Bias and Sex Fairness in Career Interest Measurement* (Washington, D.C.: U.S. Government Printing Office, 1975).

15. Alexandra P. Buek and Jeffrey H. Orlean, "Sex Discrimination–A Bar to a Democratic Education: Overview of Title IX of the Education Amendments of 1972," *Connecticut Law Review* 5 (1973): 2.

16. James A. Kelly, "Editor's Notes: The Sleeping Giant Stirs," *Rethinking*

Educational Financing: New Directions for Education (San Francisco, Calif.: Jossey-Bass, 1973), p. 3.

17. Ewald Nyquist, "Quote of the Day," *New York Times*, 9 October 1975, p. 52.

11 Affirmative Action and the Education Industry[a]

Allan C. Ornstein

Most Americans agree that the stigma of past discrimination against minorities and women must be overcome, that America is a highly polarized society, and that something must be done to increase equality and depolarization. But the increasing trend toward giving preferential treatment toward people *because* of their minority or female status is rapidly causing national controversy and uneasiness; there is concern of increasing reverse discrimination against individuals who bear no responsibility to past discrimination. A few middle-ranking bureaucrats who were never elected by the people, and who are not responsible to them, have introduced their own interpretation of the law and have imposed by fiat a quota system based on race and sex.

Guidelines originally set forth in a dispute involving construction companies in Philadelphia—where there were minority hiring problems—have been transferred from this specific situation to all institutions with government contracts of $50,000 or more or employing twenty-five or more people or both. Officials in the Department of Health, Education and Welfare have taken a plan devised for an uneducated pool of workers and proclaimed that the same minority percentages must be applied to the work force (since 1972 this has been extended to include females) in other fields such as universities, legal and medical organizations, private industry, labor unions, civil service, and others. And, if qualified persons are not available, standards must then be lowered to meet appropriate body counts. Although this chapter will focus on universities, the data are germane to nearly all sectors of the economy.

Quotas and Faculty Employment

According to federal guidelines, the goal of equal opportunity has become synonymous with equality of results for certain protest groups, who also claim to be the victims of past discrimination. With this change in the meaning of equality, the U.S. Commission on Civil Rights states that the number of minority persons found in employment at every level must be "equal to their proportions in the population."[1] In other words, the concept of equality has

[a]Portions of the first part of this paper appeared in *Phi Delta Kappan* 57 (1975): 242-245, 255.

shifted into actual employment of minorities. These minorities include blacks, persons with Spanish surnames, American Indians, Orientals, and women but not Italians, Poles, Greeks, other white ethnics, poor whites, Catholics, or Jews. Needless to say, those eligible for preferential treatment are not the only ones who have been discriminated against in the past in some way.

Applying the criterion of population proportions to jobs, the Department of Health, Education and Welfare has forced institutions of higher learning to adopt affirmative action plans that will ensure that their staffs reflect the specified balance or else be sued or lose federal funds or both. Already some universities have had their funds cut off, not because they were found guilty of specific acts of discrimination, but because their attempt to come up with an affirmative action plan did not satisfy a particular bureaucrat. Hundreds of universities have been sued, too. Their cases are pending because faculty or salary ratios were not similar—irrespective of reasons.[2]

By relying on statistical guides for ascertaining the presence of discrimination, and thus ignoring the all important criterion of qualification, the federal government is undermining the integrity and scholarly functions of universities. Some numerical targets tend to be based on body counts that are proportional to the general population; others tend to be based on the local populace. Both statistical counts are used, generally whichever is more advantageous in a given area to the minorities who are targeted for preferential treatment is chosen. But professors are not recruited from the general population (about 12 percent black) or even from the adult population (about 9 percent black) of which the black proportion is less than the total percentages. They come from the pool of college graduates with at least a master's degree and preferably a Ph.D. of which the latter percent of blacks is less than 1 percent. Indeed it is the manpower pool, not the general or adult population, that should be considered in deciding affirmative action policies; this is, in fact, true for all jobs.

In 1972 there were less than 1,500 black Ph.D.'s, not all of them in higher education. It is impossible for institutions of higher learning to have an "adequate" representation of blacks on their faculties without lowering scholastic requirements. Ironically, blacks comprise 5.5 percent of the four-year college faculties.[3] If realistic manpower pools are considered, they are already over-represented and exceed the racial balance in terms of what their formal education suggests. But HEW demands faculty percentages that correspond with population proportions. (The same twisted logic holds true for other sectors of the economy. For example, less than 2 percent of engineers are black; yet in theory Chicago engineering firms are supposed to have a 35 percent black engineering staff to reflect the surrounding population.) But it is difficult to discern whether the differential number of black-to-white academic doctorates reflect so-called racism in society, and nothing else such as cultural and family factors—the incidence of higher desertion and illegitimacy, the use of drugs, poor academic performance, and the like. Liberal and minority apologists tend to rely on "racism" to explain away all black-white differences. Any other interpretation is considered threatening, and efforts are made to limit such discussions.

A similar approach can be applied to women.[b] As many as 22 percent of all college and university teaching positions were held by women in 1972, while only 13 percent of all Ph.D.'s have been granted to women. This suggests that there are already more women on university staffs than would normally be expected. It could be argued that in the past males with the same qualifications as females have had greater opportunities in private industry and government, and thus the options of women have been constricted to university slots. This could account for some of the discrepancies in the Ph.D. pool and in the large number of female faculty members. It would certainly not illustrate university discrimination, but the opposite. Nevertheless, these institutions are being forced to make up for deficiencies that are nonexistent (if the manpower pool is considered) in the female-male, as well as the black-white, faculty ratios. Certainly there are no substantial differences in intelligence, academic talent, or scholarly potential between the sexes. It is not easy to determine whether the differential number of female-to-male academic doctorates reflect biases in graduate schools or is merely a consequence of most women devoting their energies to family life rather than careers. Nearly all Ph.D. programs have admitted candidates on a competitive basis, although some professors have rejected women in the past because of the belief that the degree would be wasted because they would eventually devote their time to marriage and raising children. Studies and statistics suggest that females feel that marriage determines the "success" of many women and that their careers are secondary. Although some feminists might claim that past restricted job opportunities for women hindered their motivation to pursue an advanced degree, and although there may be some validity to this claim, it would be difficult to show this cause-effect relationship.

Black and feminist advocates are quick to point out that their groups do not get a fair share of top positions or high salaries. This is also a misleading claim, which nonetheless gets results because of federal pressure and the apprehension of university officials to confront the charges of "racism" and "sexism." With institutions of higher learning, the general rule is that the higher positions and salaries tend to go to those who have a doctorate degree and have proven their capability and productivity over the years. We have already discussed the Ph.D. count. As for meritocracy (based on quantity), Richard Lester, in his report for the Carnegie Commission of Higher Education, has summarized several studies that show there are major differences in research and publications between men and women—a difference of about 4:1 in articles and 2:1 in books and

[b]There is no attempt to lump together blacks and women here or elsewhere in this chapter. The prospects of hiring are different for both groups, as suggested by the pool of talent, terminal degrees, and test scores. There is consistent reference to both groups because affirmative action policies are based on race and sex and seem most concerned about these two groups.

monographs—and apparently greater differences between whites and blacks.[4] Several reasons are advanced, with emphasis on the difference in societal and marriage roles between the sexes,[c] the differences in the quality of education and training, and the dual system of admitting and grading white and black college students. Hence, degrees are not equivalent.

In 1973 the male-to-female salary discrepancies were 2.5 percent in favor of men,[5] quite different from today's frequently heard charges of a salary "discrimination gap" between male and female professors. The data for salary discrepancies between races was unobtainable, although current trends suggest reverse racism. No matter how unpopular it seems, the smaller proportion of women and blacks in high paying jobs in the past, and the within-group differences for the same rank, seem to be in part a reflection of the Ph.D. qualification and professional output, and not solely a result of discrimination, as it is often alleged. Thus we come to a crucial question: Is the institution that seeks to reward merit discriminating? The enforcement procedures of the Department of Health, Education and Welfare, with their witless fervor and bigotry, say yes.

In the meantime, arbitrary "goals" and "timetables" are being imposed on institutions of higher learning by threats of reprisal. The department compliance officers usually presume the institutions guilty of discrimination against minorities and women until substantial evidence has been produced to the contrary. This reflects the biases of the investigators who are predominantly (85 percent) black or female or both,[6] with blacks occupying most of the top positions. These compliance officers also claim that certain minorities are more eligible than others for preferential treatment. They act as prosecutor, judge, and jury; they review files and records; they sometimes make outrageous demands and threaten to, and frequently, impose legal and monetary hardships. Not only do the interpretations of the executive orders (those laws that form the basis of affirmative action) continuously change, whereby institutions are often given ninety days to make "appropriate" adjustments in their numerical targets, but there is also great inconsistency among the department investigators in making their demands. Zealous threats are also made in violation of the federal guidelines. And many college administrators claim that because they are given insufficient notice of complaints filed against them, they are unable to take remedial action or defend themselves. And the courts seem to be taking the position that the accused must prove their innocence—characteristic of the inquisitorial trials of medieval Europe.[7]

---

[c]For example, female Ph.D.'s, as a group, spend an average of ten hours a week on child care plus eighteen hours a week on household chores such as cooking and cleaning, and so on. Data by both male and female researchers conclude that married women subordinate their careers to their marriage commitment. They spend less time and energy (especially research) on professional matters than men. There are other differences, such as lighter teaching loads and the assignment of graduate assistants which favor males. But these differences are slight and mainly limited to a few prestigious universities. Moreover, the latter variables may not be a function of sex but reflect differences in research and productivity.

The Department of Health, Education and Welfare has been extremely slow in approving or disapproving affirmative action plans. Delays of up to twelve to eighteen months are common, and the rejection rate is extraordinarily high. For example, up to the end of 1972 only 30 out of 197 plans were approved. For the next seven months, 3 out of 115 plans had been approved. (Data were unavailable for the remaining five months in 1973.) Between 1 January and 31 August 1974, about 20 plans were approved out of an estimated 200 submitted plans. (Here it is important to add that most of the plans were approved on the condition that further efforts be undertaken to improve minority hiring and promotions.)[8] The remarkably slow action for approving these affirmative action plans does not necessarily connote unreasonable goals and timetables. Rather, it suggests a lack of expertise within the department to judge the validity of goals for different institutions of higher learning (whose stress on merit and competence vary); the inability of the compliance officers to interpret statistical data; biases (based on sex and race) of screening committee members within the department; variation in enforcement demands at the regional and national levels (also based on the personal characteristics of the leadership at those levels); changes in regulations and laws; and the small compliance staff and the high turnover within that staff.

During a time of retrenchment and with the threat of legal action or curtailment of federal money hanging over its head, the particular university will rid itself of its potential liabilities when renegotiating with the Department of Health, Education and Welfare—that is, the practical alternative is to surrender its integrity. And, then, university officials seek to protect their jobs and limit their amount of expended energies; thus, it is common for university officials to submit to federal pressure.

The following passage from the testimony of former President James Hester of New York University before the Special Subcommittee of the U.S. Congress on Education and Labor in September 1974 illustrates the kind of problem the universities are faced with:

> Since 1968, we have been involved in at least 43 complaints before the City of New York Commission on Human Rights, the New York State Division of Human Rights, the U.S. District Court, and the EEOC. Every one of the 34 completed cases has either been dismissed, withdrawn, or results in a decision in favor of the University; nine cases are still pending.[9]

Similarly the University of Maryland, after continuous investigations by local compliance officers, which were construed as both harassment and illegal, turned around and sued the Department of Health, Education and Welfare. The result was that the department backed down from pursuing its efforts and imposing sanctions. If university officials are willing to confront the bureaucrats, they can curtail some of the mounting abuses. The examples set by New York University and the University of Maryland indicate that the department can be thwarted. But, for common sense reasons, most institutions of higher learning are reluctant to expend that kind of effort and risk the possible consequences of standing up to the federal bureaucracy. And this suggests that affirmative action may result in a stark remodeling of the criteria of professionalism and merit. In fact the point may have already been reached, according to President William J. McGill of Columbia University, where "the determination of superior ability and special excellence [is now viewed by] some officials as a mask for continuing discrimination."[10]

Officials of the Department of Health, Education and Welfare contend that absence of proportional representation of minorities and of women in an academic department reflects "exclusion" and "deficiencies." One university department found guilty can result in the entire university having its funds cut off, a twisted and dangerous example of logic. Certainly there could be a department head who discriminated and created an all majority department. However, there could also be a department head who created a predominantly or all-minority department (for example, ethnic studies, home economics, nursing). But the Department of Health, Education and Welfare is only concerned about the absence of minorities and women and usually ignores the latter department. It also fails to consider that the small size of most departments (less than 10 members) would distort the outcome of statistical analysis. Most important, since the late 1960s, the more than 2,500 institutions of higher learning awarded Ph.D.'s to only two women in meteorology; six in agronomy (crop agriculture); and less than ten (estimated) in pharmacy, nuclear chemistry, theoretical chemistry, electromagnetism, optical physics, civil engineering, and sanitary engineering. With regard to total fields during this period, women earned 0.5 percent of the Ph.D.'s in engineering, 2.3 percent in agriculture, 2.9 percent in physics, 3 percent in business administration, 3.5 percent in earth science, 4 percent in ecology, 7 percent in mathematics, and 7.6 percent in chemistry. Although the data are unavailable for blacks, the figures can be expected to be substantially lower since the *total* supply of Ph.D.'s in all fields for *all* years through 1972 was 1,500—with nearly half in the field of education.[11] Even multiplying by 1,000 the degree output each year for the subsequent five years (the period usually provided by the Department of Health, Education and Welfare to make up deficiencies) would not provide a sufficient pool of females and blacks for departments needing such personnel. Over half the departments in colleges and universities had less than fifty female doctorates and (an estimated) three black Ph.D.'s available from which to recruit during the period 1958-1967,[12] when most hiring was done in higher education. Therefore, there is no justification for listing hundreds of college and university departments as deficient. In addition, not all women and blacks with Ph.D.'s are available for posts in colleges and universities. Indeed, officials of the Department of Health, Education and Welfare need to understand that the problem is not discrimination, but the dearth of qualified people.

The department flatly denies that it is promoting a quota system, suggesting that it realizes the courts might rule against a quota system. But the distinction between "goals" and "quotas" is a matter of semantics. It would seem that the pressure tactics used by the federal government turn the goals into quotas. If low percentages of minorities and women are found to hold positions, the figure will be offered as prima facie evidence of discrimination. Using this kind of quantitative method alone, a case could be built for almost any group, not just the preferred ones. The department defends its position on the basis of compensating for past injustices, failing to recognize that it is only perpetuating other injustices.

The department, however, denies ever inferring the existence of discrimination from purely quantitative disparities between the ratios of those who apply for academic positions and those who are appointed. Nevertheless, since it requires such statistical bookkeeping, it generates pressure to hire along these bases. Moreover, compliance officials have already refused the affirmative action plans of some universities because achievement of acceptable ratios of minorities and women in academic positions was not equivalent to their availability as evidenced by the applications for employment. For example, the affirmative action plan of a large midwestern university was rejected on the ground that "the achievement of female employment in academic positions [was not] at least equivalent to their availability as evidenced by applications for employment" was not attained. And when it was pointed out by the president of a large eastern university in a predominantly white state that the number of minorities who applied for advertised positions were minimal, the compliance officer wrote back that it was the universities' responsibility "to investigate ways of improving transportation between [the closest inner city and the campus] . . . as a way of improving the minority applicant flow."

Although the department repeatedly claims that unqualified persons need not be hired, regional and local officers have instructed university administrators to "consider factors other than mere technical qualifications." What does "other than" suggest when it is necessary to comply with numerical targets? Furthermore, Revised Order No. 4, issued in April 1972, rules that it is discriminatory to require that a new applicant possess qualifications any higher than those required of "the lowest-qualified incumbent." There is no denying that universities have hired their full share of mediocrities. But rather than being permitted to upgrade the work force, universities (and other sectors of the economy) are compelled to lower standards of performance. It opens the door to the hiring of someone who cannot meet current standards or qualifications because some incumbent was hired long ago by some mistake or when standards were lower because of the scarcity of people with advanced degrees or when the institution was struggling for recognition. In effect, the government has applied Gresham's law to the universities (and elsewhere in the job sector). The result is bound to have a downgrading effect in hiring and promoting personnel. In addition, the department now insists that an institution "may hold certain vacancies open until such time as qualified minorities are found and considered." This has the same effect of excluding nonminorities and also forces institutions to hire *qualifiable* (not yet qualified) minority group personnel, since they cannot indefinitely keep a position vacant without loosing the line position. It is easier for an institution to hire a qualifiable person who fills a quota than to explain why someone could not be found and risk federal reprisal.

As a result, universities have openly indicated to placement bureaus and candidates that they are interested in hiring *only* minorities and females, preferably black females. For example, a large state university on the West Coast told placement bureaus across the country that it was now seeking "an employee balance which is in ethnic and male/female groups, approximate that of the population of the . . . area from which we recruit. What this means is that we have shifted from the idea of equal opportunity in employment to a deliberate effort to seek out qualified and *qualifiable* [not yet qualified] people among ethnic minority groups and women to fill *all* jobs." And a nearby college has advertised: "We desire to appoint a black or Chicano, preferably female." The department head of a large southwestern university responded to an inquiry of the placement bureau of another university, stating that although the "four candidates seem qualified for a vacancy they cannot be considered" because every effort must be made "to recruit a minority person." He pointed out that his university recruiting policies had changed and he was "*no longer [able to] seek the best-qualified* person available, regardless of race, color, or creed, as in the past." The president of a Midwestern city college system whose faculty was more than 12 percent black, informed his various administrators that they must hire additional minority faculty members. When the year ends, he said, "many qualified whites will not be rehired and blacks will be sought to fill their jobs." At one of the more than seventy units of the largest state system on the East Coast, a similar directive informs the vice-presidents, dean, and department heads that for the next five years existing vacancies will go to "*qualifiable* persons on the basis of race and sex . . . [A]nd temporary preferences [will be given] . . . to members of minority groups." Further, this hiring is to be on a "three-to-one ratio for professors" and a "one-to-one hiring of minorities affecting all of the administrative staff." And the president of a prestigious university on the East Coast sent a directive to his line administrators about a "new and innovative program to help achieve affirmative action," which includes the "hiring of *unqualified* and *marginally qualified* people."[13]

Thus we can appreciate the findings of Stuart Gould and Pierre Van Den Berghe, who, with fictitious resumes, each applied for teaching posts in sociology to 176 universities. Their applications were identical except that one applicant was identified as male and the other as female. Half of all the applicants were described as black; and the other half made no mention of race. Ninety-six institutions replied. Sex did not affect the response rate, suggesting that it is important in only certain fields. But the response rate to the black applicant was 61 percent; to the applicant whose race was not listed, 48 percent. More important, 44 percent expressed follow-up interest in the black applicant, only 9.5 percent in the other applicant (significant at the .001 level). Conclusion: blacks have a decided edge in today's job market.[14]

Considering the university job market as a whole, it is reported that black professors accuse white women of being aggressive and deflecting attention away from correcting racism. There are counter charges by white women that few blacks have the formal credentials for faculty appointments and that those who are qualified or even qualifiable are hired and able to command higher salaries than their white male and female counterparts because of supply and demand.[15] A similar dispute between blacks and white women over the spoils system of "reform" is also evident in private industry and government.[16] And Lester concludes that institutions of higher learning are pirating the limited number of qualified minority and women faculty members from each other, offering higher salaries than those given to comparable and more competent nonminorities and men. Some of the preferred groups lack proper qualifications for the positions, sometimes tenured positions, to which they are appointed. Lester warns that present minority (and in some cases female) hiring trends are hurting standards and undermining faculty quality. He also indicates that salaries between blacks and whites favor the former and run between $3,000 to $4,000 at the assistant rank and as high as $8,000 at the associate and full-professor rank.[17] His statistics are based on pre-1970 data, when affirmative action was in its infancy. The income differences is probably greater today.

Although report after report tell of a Ph.D. glut, there seems to be no problem for a black Ph.D. to find a job. While many whites with the same degree (including females in some academic areas) are underemployed or unable to find jobs in their fields of specialization, blacks (and Chicanos) are receiving several offers with starting salaries that frequently exceed $20,000.[18] The average starting salary for a Ph.D. is about $12,000; $20,000 is comparable to what the average full professor earns after ten years.[19] These trends may reflect the law of supply and demand. But many would say that the different salary pattern reverse discrimination and is grounds for legal action.

Still another interesting twist is that many minorities have discovered a valuable strategy for advancement. In a period of university retrenchment, when few promotions and salary raises are forthcoming, minority and women faculty have threatened to and actually filed complaints of discrimination. With the aid of government pressure, they receive special salary differentials as well as an extra share of the limited pie.[d] And it has become increasingly difficult to discharge a

[d]For example, one university in Arizona has made available a bonus fund to pay minorities an extra $750 a year over their white counterparts. At a southside Chicago state university more than $1,000 was paid across the board to all black and female faculty members, even to those already earning $25,000 and $30,000, to compensate for past discrimination. At another private university in Illinois, a number of female faculty members filed a class action suit in order to pressure the university to promote them.

"preferred" person, even if incompetent because most institutions are already under the gun for alleged "deficiencies" that must be "corrected."

What does all this mean? Besides the obvious political ramifications, colleges and universities (and other sectors of the economy) are no longer hiring or promoting the most qualified candidates. They are instead hiring minorities from a limited and sometimes qualifiable pool, and at unusually high salaries, to fill quotas. To require institutions to commit themselves to achieving a certain proportion of minorities and women on their faculties is to prevent them from choosing the most qualified individuals. It mocks academic standards and it generates hostility and bitterness among more qualified individuals who must be paid less or passed over. Although universities may be required to implement such a policy to reduce racial polarization and to produce equal results, the present affirmative action program has produced a new kind of social welfare program that should not be considered performance- nor quality-based. Less competent people cannot compete because they have been situated at a level beyond their capacities. This is bound to create self-doubt and frustration among them. But it also reveals a racism within the liberal community which excuses the incompetence as if it was the best that could be produced by the minority community.

Surely there is need to reduce racial polarization, and some kind of affirmative action plan may be necessary to bridge the existing chasm. But the problem lies with the officials who administer and interpret the present program. They are an indigenous group of civil servants trained in bureaucratic modes of organization who are promulgating regulations on institutions, aided and abetted by a small group of evangelistic crusaders who are presaging a new kind of racism. This is creating new injustices and new hostilities and elevating the hypocrisy of egalitarian reform, which condemns superior ability and high standards as "a mask for continuing discrimination."

Quotas and Student Admissions

Across the country similar quotas are being established for admission into colleges and universities; a dual system of admissions for black and white students, which in turn is producing a dual system of grading. Reformers have come to despair the ability of black Americans to better themselves educationally, even when special programs and monies are provided. Compensatory education has been assessed as a failure, and the politics of protest now demands "new standards" for minorities so as to guarantee equality. The concept of equal opportunity has been transformed into the ideology of equal results—at the expense of standards of excellence. In line with this new policy, most colleges and universities are asking student applicants to "voluntarily" respond to a supplementary civil rights questionnaire. The applicant indicates if he belongs to a minority or nonminority group. It can be assumed that a minority applicant gladly fills in the questionnaire, almost guaranteeing himself admission. It is usually taken for granted that the individual who does not volunteer the information is white. Some admission forms now require a photograph, a return of the pre-1954 *Brown* decision, only in reverse—to limit whites.

The kind of pressure that the universities are faced with is illustrated by a communication to a western university. It was charged with discrimination against minorities because in one department "out of many applicants only one minority person was enrolled [for the term]." Another illustration is a compliance letter to an Ivy league university which demanded to know why there were no minority students in the Graduate Department of Religious Studies. The department head responded that a reading knowledge of Latin, Greek, or Hebrew was required. The Department of Health, Education and Welfare representative advised: "then end those old fashioned programs that require irrelevant languages. And start up programs or relevant things which minority group students can study without learning languages." Clearly, the situation has become irresponsible. Two leading black social scientists, Martin Kilson from Harvard University and Thomas Sowell from UCLA, point out that the Scholastic Aptitude Test and Graduate Record Examination scores for most entering blacks (even at the prestigious universities) are now in the 25th percentile on a national level. Such students are occupying seats that would normally require scores above the 90th percentile.[20] On a nationwide basis, a recent study by the Association of American Law Schools reports that all but two of fifty law schools surveyed indicated preferential treatment and the lowering of admission standards toward minorities.[21] Similarly, Jack Shepard indicates that by 1971, 79 out of 100 medical schools reported that admission requirements were being lowered to admit additional minorities. More women were being admitted into medical schools, but their scores were similar to those of white males.[22] The point is, a great many seats are being reserved for minority students whose formal qualifications are questionable. Moreover, seats are being taken away from more qualified students.

For example, Stanford University Law School virtually guaranteed admission in 1972 to any minority student whose grade point average was not below that of the lowest scoring white in the 1971 class and whose Law School Admission Test (LSAT) was within fifty points of that of the weakest student in the previous entering class. In 1973 Northwestern Law School was admitting blacks who scored below the 10th percentile on the LSAT, some of whom were from colleges whose accreditation was under question. The school was, at the same time, refusing admission to white students who scored in the 80th and 90th percentiles. The University of Illinois Medical School at Urbana reserved 60 out of 300 places in its incoming class for minorities in 1972. More recently, the University of California Medical School at Davis set aside 10 percent of its seats for minorities. On the campus of the California State University at Fresno, the goals for the 1972 graduate class in social work were to admit "one-third black, one-third Chicano, one-tenth other minorities, and the remainder Caucasian students." These examples are only the tip of the iceberg; they are sentiments that can seriously erode the quality of higher education under the guise of "reform."

The DeFunis case is perhaps the best known example of a student denied admission because of preferential treatment given to minorities. DeFunis, white, with an A average, applied to the Washington University Law School in 1971 and was rejected. He later discovered that thirty-eight other applicants, all minorities, with lower grades and lower LSAT scores were accepted. DeFunis sued the university, charging he was the victim of reverse discrimination. He won his case in the state court and was admitted; the decision was overturned in the federal district court in 1973. The case reached the U.S. Supreme Court in 1974. In a seven-page unsigned opinion, with four justices dissenting, the Court ruled that the issue was moot; any decision reached by the Court would have been made after DeFunis had finished his studies. The dissenting judges argued that DeFunis was still in his last year of law school and still could be subject to a number of unexpected events that might prevent him from graduating. He thus might be faced with another admissions rejection. But most important to the dissenting judges was their belief that the case was not moot for a vast number of other students, and therefore the issue should be resolved for the interests of the public. (Here it can be assumed that a large number of students have had no idea that they were victimized by a quota system and so did not pursue their cases in the courts.) The nondecision of the DeFunis case evoked considerable criticism, and it certainly did not resolve the problem. In 1974 a rejected white medical student at the University of Illinois at Urbana and another at University of California Davis filed similar lawsuits.

The question eventually arises: To what extent are we supposed to discriminate against high-achieving students, even those who are from groups that have also known harsh discrimination but have nevertheless done well in school and in various areas of employment? Nathan Glazer touches on this question, reporting on several prominent studies by sociologists, anthropologists, and psychologists; he contends that:

> History and social research convince me there are deep and enduring educational differences between various ethnic groups, in their educational achievement and in the broader cultural characteristics in which these differences are, I believe, rooted; that these differences cannot be simply associated with the immediate conditions under which these groups live, whether we define these conditions as being those of levels of poverty and exploitation, or prejudice and discrimination; and if we are to have a decent society, men must learn to live with some measure of group difference in educational achievement, [and] to tolerate them. . . .[23]

Glazer is concerned about society's attitudes toward those differences: Are they solely the consequence of the ill will and "racist" feelings of teachers, administrators, social scientists, and society in general? About the differences he asks, "How elaborate are we to make the efforts to wipe them out, and how successful can we hope to be no matter how elaborate our efforts are? Are our measures to equalize to include the restriction of the opportunities of those groups that seem to find school achievement easy?"[24]

And a related question is: To what extent are we supposed to ignore, even penalize, ordinary students and less-than-average students who are white and come from poor, working, or middle-class backgrounds? No one asks whether a black or Chicano applicant came from a home more advantaged than some white person seeking admission into college or applying for the same job. Thus Paul Seabury cites the frustration of one white person from a poor background:

> The ability to think in the abstract is hard for a person with my cultural background and economic background. My parents' . . . income barely exceeded the poverty level. My father is a Southern Baptist with a third-grade education . . . I believe I am a victim. As a nonmember of a minority group I feel that I . . . [am] discriminated against constantly. The same admission standards are not applied because a certain percentage of minority students must be admitted in each class regardless of their qualifications. My test scores, undergraduate record, and my family (poor white) deny me admittance to Harvard because I am white.[25]

In reality, both the high-achieving and ordinary white students are going to suffer. They are going to pay the social costs and carry the burden of those of their elders who profited from the old patterns of discrimination. This is, of course, unfair to the present generation of young whites, especially white males. But the greater damage will be that their brotherhood and goodwill will quickly be eroded by the kind of discrimination others have so valiantly fought. Many of these young students must make room for less capable students. Who is going to compensate them for their eventual underemployment and "nouveau poverty"?

Today there is little tolerance for group differences. Yet, all groups *are* different—some groups are better achievers, some are average achievers, and some are less-than-average achievers. But the egalitarians prefer to fit everyone into their imaginary bell-shaped curves and mask whatever differences may exist among racial and ethnic groups. One who believes in equality treats a person, not as a member of a group, but as an individual. A belief in equality depends, not on the notion that all groups are equal, but on the idea that all groups be treated equally. The latter philosophy also recognizes that people are not born equal, that they are unique and possess different abilities and capacities to learn. What equality means is that individuals should be offered equal protection of the law and equal right to fulfill their unique potentialities, that they should be treated with equal dignity and value as human beings. Paul Kurtz writes, "One who believes in equality need not insist that all individuals, races, or ethnic groups are exactly alike in every way."[26] And Sidney Hook contends, "Our democratic commitment depends on providing equal opportunity for all persons . . . to develop themselves to the fullest." There must be "the recognition and appreciation of the importance of individual differences," which does not depend on the belief that all groups are the same.[27]

Most would agree they want those qualified students to attend colleges, universities, and professional schools who have a reasonable degree of literacy and who can understand their textbooks. Otherwise there is a regression effect down to the new mean in standards and grades. Moreover, the terminal degree becomes meaningless and especially suspect for minorities who represent a quota, including those who are able students. Thus, under the guise of removing arbitrary barriers that impede the progress of minorities, some students are admitted into college who are functional illiterates.[28] They cannot write a complete sentence nor read above the fifth grade level.[29] Not only do most of them graduate, they also apply considerable pressure on administrators and faculty to expand their enrollment.[30] If the university's mission is to be nothing more than a social action agency, or if the demise of academic standards is fostered in order for society to pay its "reparations" and meet its social responsibilities, then the world of higher education is bankrupt. All the excuses and rhetoric conjured up for abandoning academic quality will not make the new anti-intellectual atmosphere go away, even if the relaxed admissions and grading criteria benefits many nonminority students. But so long as high standards are seen by many blacks as "culturally biased" or manifestations of "white supremacy," black students will continue to be perceived as less than qualified and, in turn, so will those who become professors. Reminders that black entry into the American intellectual mainstream depends on encouraging and holding to high standards of educational excellence continue to be misunderstood by many blacks. So long as it does, the image of black academic identity will continue to suffer.

A double standard already exists in grading blacks and whites in institutions of higher learning. It predominates at all levels and in all fields of study, including Ph.D. programs and law and medical schools. By admitting weak students, the system becomes susceptible to accusations of "racism," "discrimination," and legal action if it attempts to maintain standards.[31] Hence, there is pressure on many white professors to dilute their grading system for nonwhite students. It is often not worth the personal costs and potential harassment to grade all students on the same basis, and far too many minority students would fail.[32] But there also is administrative pressure not to fail minority students who represent a quota or open admission policy. A large number of such students dropout on their own accord, and university administrators are often reluctant to maintain standards and thus increase the dropout figures among these academically weak students.[33] Minority students quickly perceive the benefits of the new grading system and also become sophisticated in challenging professors who attempt to maintain standards. The students invent stories or just pressure the professor, which frequently leads to grade changes. In the long run, this procedure is bound to effect the self-esteem of minority students, and not only those who are academically weak. Those of high ability, who excel strictly on merit, will carry the stigma that they, too, were beneficiaries of a double standard, not to mention how it will affect students who graduate without favoritism.

One of the best-known examples of such pressure tactics occurred at Wayne State University. Several black students, at the end of their freshman year, were notified by the law school of their dismissal for academic failure. They chained themselves to the doorpost and refused to leave, charging that the university had discriminated against them. The professors denied the charge and responded that test papers were identified by number, not the student's name. A few faculty even said that if they had known which papers were submitted by black students, they would have leaned over backward to help them attain a passing grade. The law school eventually agreed to permit the students to remain. Similar incidents have occurred at various universities, sometimes involving individual students and sometimes, groups of students. In effect, then, graduation will not guarantee equality of academic outcome or professional competence.

But those who have benefited from less rigorous college standards and testing scales often must compete on professional licensing examinations with those who were not favored. For example, a disproportionately high number of black students who succeed in obtaining their law degrees have difficulty passing state law boards. In Michigan the 1971 results showed that the passing rate was 71 percent for whites and 17 percent for blacks. A law suit has been filed in Michigan, claiming that the test is "culturally biased" against blacks. Between 1970 and 1973, only 22 percent of the whites taking the Illinois law boards failed; among blacks, 55 percent did not pass. A law suit which claims "discrimination" has been filed in Illinois, too. In 1972 Pennsylvania revised its bar examination so that candidates who pass either a multiple choice or essay section (which had been a stumbling block to blacks) were considered to have passed. And one bar association, composed mainly of black lawyers, has called for the abolition of the bar examination in all states because they claim the tests are biased.

The medical profession is experiencing the same kind of pressure. Having changed their entrance standards to increase black enrollments in the medical colleges, at its 1973 annual convention in Philadelphia, the American Medical Association debated the validity of the medical examinations and whether it should be required for students who succeed in obtaining their degrees. There is strong pressure by a consortium of liberal-minority groups to eliminate such exams all together. The contention is that the person who receives a degree from an accredited medical school should be admitted into practice without further ado. In Chicago prospective teachers who wish to avoid taking or who have failed the relatively simple multiple-choice National Teacher Examination may substitute three years of experience and become permanently certified. The result is that many Chicago teachers "can't spell," and are reading at "the fifth to sixth grade level."[34]

In the meantime, the NAACP (and other civil rights organizations) has successfully argued in the courts in such cities as Boston, New York City, Detroit, Chicago, and San Francisco that the written examinations used to select and promote teachers, firemen, and policemen are "biased" and discriminate against minorities, especially blacks. Moreover, the U.S. Supreme Court has ruled in *Griggs* v. *Duke Power* (1971) that tests can no longer be considered a reasonable job requirement for minorities. All arbitrary barriers to unemployment that demand certain skills or test score results and have the effect of employing minorities in less than their proportion to the population are now considered illegal. If test scores are involved, the employer must now demonstrate that the tests are a valid predictor of job success. That the employer has no discriminatory intention is irrelevant; it is only the effect that matters now. The *Griggs* decision is not aimed at helping white women who fall under affirmative action guidelines or helping poor or ethnic whites who do not speak fluent English. The decision applies to only certain minorities who seem unable to compete on cognitive tests. The Court claimed that tests are biased and that they are not an accurate predictor of job success. But the decision was not related to the technical nature of the tests, for there are many highly reliable and valid predictors of achievement and job performance. As Jerome Dopplet and George Bennett of the Psychological Corporation report, there are some technical limitations to tests. But there are many well-devised (reliable and valid) tests that measure "the individual's present capacity of demonstrating his skills or knowledge for predicting job success."[35] The concept of "cultural bias" entered the picture to mask the politics of the decision—to provide jobs on a quota basis and to eliminate any tool, such as tests to determine appropriate skills and professional competency, that might hinder the quota policy.

The combined implications of the NAACP strategy and the *Griggs* decision make it clear that conventional criteria for judging performance and potential in all jobs are under attack—that is, any job-related skills, such as required for university publication record or terminal degree; for position; knowledge of a profession (teaching, law, medicine), as measured by standardized tests; a secretary's ability to read and type; or a bank clerk's ability to do simple mathematical problems, are being attacked.

Tests may be culturally oriented, but the job is embedded in a cultural milieu. Similarly, the ability to write a Ph.D. thesis or conduct research for a professor is not a racially-biased requirement. Nor is it racially biased for a history teacher to have knowledge of history or a lawyer to have knowledge of law or the secretary to understand written instructions, or the bank teller to know how to add and subtract. These are culturally laden factors which are likely to be criteria, or job related. The purpose of a test is to select people who will succeed on the job. Outlawing such tests makes the selection process more subjective and political. It is not possible to claim that all high school or college diplomas are equivalent, or that graduation from a school of law, medicine, or education is sufficient indication of competence. Certifying examinations are necessary. Eliminating them denies that there are dual entrance and grading systems for black and white students, and that within groups there are other large differences. The result is that these differences are perpetuated on the job. Hence, many functional illiterates are graduated from high school, and many students with less than average qualifications are now admitted into colleges and professional schools. When these students go out on the job, ironically, they transfer the blame for their failures from schools and teachers to the qualifying tests that reflect the different outcomes in diplomas. Dopplet and Bennett put it this way: "Whenever the number of applicants exceeds the number of job openings, some applicants will be rejected. This is one of the hard facts of life. It is not surprising that those who are rejected sometimes attack the selection procedures on the grounds that these are invalid or unfair."[36]

Society has the responsibility for providing jobs for people with limited skills, but not for replacing qualified personnel with unqualified personnel. Society has the responsibility of providing remedial job instruction for disadvantaged populations, but should also include white disadvantaged populations. The rejection of measurements that register the consequences of educational deprivation or of inadequate knowledge and skills, is merely a political move to kill off the messenger who brings the bad news. It deemphasizes the harsh reality that quotas will lead to a downward trend in the quality and abilities of people who are and will be employed in a variety of jobs and occupations. New and artificial standards that mock excellence and replace it with mediocrity have little to do with equal opportunity. Using quotas, instead of quality, to select people for college entrance or for jobs and promotions rewards the dumb, lazy, and unambitious at the expense of the smart, talented, and ambitious. But the philosophical and ethnic arguments that are devised are secondary. The political decision to absorb selected groups into society in line with the egalitarian demand for equal results is a larger part of the rationale for the quota decision.

Conclusion

A qualified surgeon is expected when an operation must be performed, yet there are quotas in medical schools. Seats are reserved for *qualifiable* students and taken from the more qualified. A skilled lawyer is wanted when a legal matter must be handled, yet there are quotas for candidates applying to law schools. A skilled pilot and flight mechanic are required to service airplanes, yet the airlines are coming under pressure to fill quotas. Universities want high standards of scholarship and excellence, yet they are not permitted to hire or promote the most qualified. There may be nothing wrong with producing ordinary doctors, lawyers, pilots, and professors. But there is a point beyond which the definition of "average" can be stretched so that it does serious harm to the viability of society.

Despite the various legal and moral convictions, it takes several years to educate people and turn out qualified professionals for important vocations. No increased pressure is going to increase the supply of doctors and lawyers and such, unless standards are lowered. Instant competency cannot be bestowed. Already qualified minority group members and women are becoming uneasy about quotas. They are aware that it puts a "less qualified" stamp on them by association. Within a few years it can be expected that people will be asking, "How did that person get the job? Besides filling a quota, does that person have any legitimate qualifications?" If the question of competency is not seriously considered, or if such matters no longer count, there will be a decline in public and private services. Although there is less concern about efficiency in some jobs than in others, the placement of less efficient personnel at low levels will raise costs and diminish standards. To what extent each institution can absorb less efficient personnel without disabling itself or without becoming another post office is a difficult question to answer.

The present use of quotas is only part of the issue. It should not be permitted to mask the larger issue—the danger of a de facto system of quotas, a rigid system that leaves no room for maneuver and that is bound to be a denial of equal opportunity. While special efforts should be made to identify and train individuals of minority status, and other programs are needed to assist potentially qualified minorities, essential prerequisites and criteria of excellence cannot be dropped for an extended period without serious social and economic repercussions. The more the importance of merit and ability is diminished, the greater the danger of a decline of society. Abolishing standardized tests, eliminating examinations, bending entrance requirements (for college and employment), downgrading skills or doing away with them, or denying quantitative measures of excellence are wrong and antiintellectual. Being unable to test for competency, because of so-called cultural biases, is highly political and eliminates any tool to distinguish the qualified from the unqualified, the competent from the incompetent, and all under the guise of affirmative action.

There are those who feel the present affirmative action policy is just, especially those who benefit from it. They, along with their liberal apologists, will disagree with this analysis. But certainly there is need to deal with a greater sense of reality. Who is supposed to share the blame for past injuries? Can we accurately determine who should be penalized? What is the present trade-off between increasing minority employment and decreasing efficiency? How do we assist underprivileged whites? Or, do we continue to ignore them? Are all women included in affirmative action? Or does it mainly apply to selected fields and minority women? Where do the benefits of civil rights begin to fall off and lead to abuses toward the majority population? When do the arbitrary interpretations of a few unelected officials become a matter for the people to check?

The future is now. White males will begin to file reverse discrimination law suits when they compare their formal qualifications with "preferred" candidates and the recent salaries offered and obtained by minority counterparts with their own salaries. Letters of "no openings" to white candidates will be matched with invitations to minority candidates. White students will learn the advantage of claiming minority status when filling out forms for law, medical, and graduate school. They may eventually file suit against universities for discrimination in the allotment of financial aid (and jobs on campus), showing that many minorities who receive financial assistance come from families with higher incomes than their own.

In the final analysis, ideological imperatives and group interests should not prevail over the norms of the legal order and individual rights. Somehow a balance must be struck between the entitlements from those groups that now claim special privilege and other groups whose rights must not be abridged. Individual merit, measured as accurately as possible, must be a crucial determinant in educational and employment opportunities, rather than proportional representation. A double-standard society will not work for long, and it will breed new racial antagonisms.

Notes

1. U.S. Commission on Civil Rights, *Federal Civil Rights Enforcement Effort* (Washington, D.C.: U.S. Government Printing Office, 1970).

2. U.S., Congress, Senate, *Congressional Record* 119 (22, May 1973); Paul Seabury, "HEW and the Universities," *Commentary* 55 (1972): 33-44.

3. Alan E. Bayer, *Teaching Faculty in Academe: 1972-73*, American Council on Education Research Report, vol. 8 (Washington, D.C.: American Council on Education, 1973).

4. Richard A. Lester, *Antibias Regulation of Universities* (New York: McGraw-Hill, 1974).

5. *Chronicle of Higher Education*, 5 August 1974, p. 9.

6. Lester, *Antibias Regulation of Universities.*

7. Allan C. Ornstein, *Race and Politics in School Community Organizations* (Pacific Palisades, Calif.: Goodyear, 1974); idem, "Are Quotas Here to Stay in Minority Hiring?" *National Review*, 26 April 1974, pp. 478-479ff; Sheldon E. Steinbach, "Fighting Campus Job Discrimination," *Change* 5 (November 1973): 51-52.

8. Letter to Sheldon Steinbach of the American Council on Education from Gwendolyn H. Gregory, director of the Office of Policy Communication, Office for Civil Rights, 17 September 1973; Lester, *Antibias Regulation of Universities*; *Chronicle of Higher Education*, 27 January 1975, p. 6; ibid., 19 May 1975, p. 43; and telephone conversation with Miro M. Todorovich, coordinator of the Committee on Academic Nondiscrimination and Integrity, 17 February 1975.

9. James Hester, Statement before the Special Subcommittee on Education and Labor, Congress of the United States, September 20, 1974.

10. *New York Times*, 7 May 1972, p. 12.

11. Commission on Human Resources, National Research Council, *Summary Reports, 1967-1973: Doctorate Recipients from United States Universities* (Washington, D.C.: National Academy of Sciences, 1967-1974).

12. Commission on Human Resources, National Research Council, *Doctorate Recipients from United States Universities, 1958-1966* (Washington, D.C.: National Academy of Sciences, 1967); Miro M. Todorovich, Statement before the Special Subcommittee on Education and Labor, Congress of the United States, 20 September 1974.

13. U.S., Congress, Senate, *Congressional Record* 119 (May 22, 1973); Ornstein, *Race and Politics* (italics added throughout). For additional letters, see these two sources.

14. Stuart H. Gould and Pierre L. Van Den Berghe, "Particularism in Sociology Departments' Hiring Practices," *Race* 15 (1973): 106-111.

15. *Chronicle of Higher Education*, 23 October 1973, pp. 1-6; ibid., 5 August 1974, pp. 1, 8-9.

16. *Chicago Tribune*, 2 December 1973, sec. 12, p. 35; ibid., 4 March 1974, sec. 2, p. 9; Jules Cohen, "Coping with Affirmative Action against Backlash," *Business and Society Review*, 4 (1973): 32-36; *New York Times*, 30 September 1974, p. 28; Daniel Seligman, "How 'Equal Opportunity' Turned into Employment Quotas," *Fortune*, 87 (March 1973): 160-168.

17. Lester, *Antibias Regulation of Universities.*

18. *Chicago Sun-Times*, 4 September 1973, p. 38.

19. *Chronicle of Higher Education*, 29 April 1974, p. 9.

20. Martin T. Kilson, "The Black Experience at Harvard," *New York Times Magazine*, 2 September 1973, pp. 13, 31ff.; Thomas A. Sowell, *Black Education: Myths and Tragedies* (New York, McKay, 1974).

21. Committee on Academic Nondiscrimination and Integrity, "Statement for Immediate Release," 9 June 1972.

22. Jack Shephard, "Black Lab Power," *Saturday Review*, 5 August 1972; pp. 32-35ff.

23. Nathan Glazer, "Ethnic Group and Education: Toward the Tolerance of Difference," *Journal of Negro Education* 38 (1969): 187.

24. Ibid., p. 194.

25. Seabury, "HEW and the Universities," p. 44.

26. Paul Kurtz, "The Principle of Equality and Some Dogmas of Environmentalism," *Humanist* 32 (March 1972): 4.

27. Sidney Hook, "Democracy and Genetic Variation," *Humanist* 32 (March 1972): 7.

28. Bernard Bard, "College for All: Dream or Disaster?" *Phi Delta Kappan* 56 (1975): 219.

29. *Chicago Sun-Times*, 15 January 1975, p. 48; *Chicago Tribune*, 29 November 1974, sec. 2, p. 2; Orde Coombs, "The Necessity of Excellence: Howard University," *Change* 6 (March 1974): 36-41; Louis G. Heller, *The Death of the American University* (New York: Arlington House, 1974).

30. David L. Kirp and Mark G. Yudof, "DeFunis and Beyond," *Change* 6 (November 1974): 22-28; Sowell, *Black Education.*

31. Kilson, "Black Experience at Harvard." Also see Martin Kilson, review of "The Education of Black Folk" by Allen B. Ballard, *Change* 5 (November 1973): 58-60; Sowell, *Black Education.*

32. Wilson Record, "Can Sociology and Black Studies Find a Common Ground?" (Paper presented at the Black Cultural Forum, Portland State University, February 1973); idem, "Response of Sociologists to Black Studies," in *Black Sociologists: Historical and Contemporary Perspectives*, ed. J.E. Blackwell and Morris Janowitz (Chicago: University of Chicago Press, 1974), pp. 368-401; Bayard Ruston, ed., *Black Studies: Myths and Realities* (New York: A. Philip Randolph Educational Fund, 1969). Also see Edward M. White, "Sometimes an A is Really an F," *Chronicle of Higher Education*, 3 February 1975, p. 24.

33. Martin Mayer, "Higher Education for All?" *Commentary* 56 (February 1973): 37-47.

34. *Chicago Tribune*, 18 September 1974, pp. 1, 15. It is also reported by the city's black newspaper that about half the number of Chicago's 27,000 teachers, most of whom are black, earn their degrees at one southside university. In 1973 as many as 63 percent of the 827 teacher candidates at this institution failed the National Teacher Examination but were still eligible to teach. See the *Chicago Defender*, 30 March 1974, pp. 1, 9ff.

35. Jerome E. Dopplet and George K. Bennett, "Testing Job Applicants from Disadvantaged Groups," *Test Service Bulletin of the Psychological Corporation*, no. 57 (1967), p. 1.

36. Ibid., p. 5.

About the Editors

Allan C. Ornstein received the Ph.D. from New York University. He is a Fulbright-Hayes scholar and professor of education at Loyola University of Chicago. His consultant work is varied and includes work for the Educational Testing Service, American Federation of Teachers, American Educational Research Association, U.S. Congress, New York and Illinois state departments of education, and New York-Chicago-Evanston-Montreal school boards. Dr. Ornstein is the author of more than 100 articles and 14 books. Among his recent books are: *Race and Politics in School/Community Organizations* (1974), *Reforming Metropolitan Schools* (1975), *The Paraprofessional's Handbook* (1975), *Teaching in a New Era* (1976) and *Introduction to the Foundations of Education* (scheduled for January of 1977).

Steven I. Miller received the Ph.D. from Michigan State University. He is an assistant professor of educational foundations at Loyola University of Chicago. His major research interests have centered around the relationship of social research and social policy, and models of social mobility as they relate to inequality of educational opportunity. Dr. Miller's most recent articles have appeared in the *Journal of Law and Education* and *Quality and Quantity: The American-European Journal of Methodology.* He has also completed a text manuscript in the Sociology of Education to appear this year.

LA
210
.P64